Reiki

From **BEGINNER**
to **PRACTITIONER**

Jacqueline Raison

From **BEGINNER**
to **PRACTITIONER**

THE CROWOOD PRESS

First published in 2022 by
The Crowood Press Ltd
Ramsbury, Marlborough
Wiltshire SN8 2HR

enquiries@crowood.com

www.crowood.com

British Library Cataloguing-in-Publication Data
A catalogue record for this book is available from the British Library.

ISBN   978 0 7198 4083 8

Cover design: Sergey Tsvetkov

'If Reiki can be spread throughout the world
It will touch the human heart and the morals of society.
It will be helpful for many people,
Not only healing disease, but
The Earth as a whole.'

Extract from the engraving on Mikao Usui's memorial stone.

Typeset by Chennai Publishing Services

Printed and bound in India by Parksons Graphics

CONTENTS

ACKNOWLEDGEMENTS

My greatest thanks go to Reiki Master Teacher Gaynor Mentiply who first introduced me to Reiki. As a psychic medium she might have been aware of just how much my life would change as a result, but if she did, she didn't let on! And then my greatest love and respect must go to my Reiki Master Teacher Tina Reibl, who taught me the Reiki Master Teacher level whilst on retreat in Japan, the single most illuminating week of my life.

Sincere thanks to Susan Edmunson, who tirelessly read all my drafts, for her inspiration and support, and to the wonderful Vicky Banning, who as well as reading the drafts managed to keep The Reiki School running whilst I was absorbed in writing.

Many, many thanks to my family, who with one voice say that they like me much more as a Reiki teacher than they ever did as a lawyer! Particularly to my husband, Gordon, for his continuous support and encouragement and for modelling for some of the photos, stepson Andrew for patiently explaining string theory and other quantum physics concepts to me, son Matthew for endless encouragement, step-daughter Kate for discussions on the NHS and mental health, daughter Hannah for reading the first draft and for modelling for many of the photos, to step-daughter Alex for being my first and most encouraging Reiki patient and to Corinne, daughter-in-law-to-be, for typing the first few chapters. Also to James and Flynn at Wessex Working Horses.

And finally, my thanks to my publisher. I had no intention of writing a book on Reiki, but they approached me at the beginning of the first Covid-19 lockdown, and, as I was unable to teach, this book became my lifeline through those times.

INTRODUCTION

I first came across Reiki while browsing in a crystal shop near Oxford. Despite a successful career as a commercial lawyer, a supportive husband and a wonderful family, I still felt that something was missing in my life. I had been interested in holistic healing for over twenty years, an interest I credit to the National Childbirth Trust, who encouraged mothers to take responsibility for their pregnancy, and to the extent possible, labour. Matthew was born with a vitamin K deficiency, for which he was given injections into his heel from almost the moment he was born. This was an upsetting intervention to our otherwise natural birth experience, and led me to research forms of complementary therapy that I could use safely with my children.

I started studying homeopathy whilst on maternity leave. It suited my logical lawyer brain. After that, I started to combine my love of gardening with my interest in healing, creating herbal remedies from plants in my garden. I went on to learn dowsing, the Silva Method and crystal healing. But it was when I discovered Reiki that my life started to change in quite remarkable ways.

I took my Reiki Master Teacher level as a week-long retreat in Kyoto, Japan. At the time I had no intention of teaching, but fairly soon after I took my Masters I was able to leave my full-time job as a commercial lawyer and set up as a consultant, effectively working as a lawyer three days per week, enabling me to work with Reiki the other four.

When my Reiki Master Tina wanted to retire she asked me if I had an interest in taking over the Reiki School, and after working with her as an apprentice for a year I did so. I now run the Reiki School full time, teaching in the UK and Japan, running workshops and retreats. It is my soul's purpose to introduce as many people to Reiki as possible, and to do it in such a way that they use Reiki frequently in their daily lives. I sincerely hope that this book is another way of reaching people and introducing them to Reiki.

The Approaches I have taken in this Book

When teaching Reiki it is impossible to ignore the spiritual dimension. Reiki does not associate with any religion and followers of all religions (or no religion) successfully work with Reiki. I have used the terms 'God', 'Source' and 'Universe' interchangeably to reflect the inclusive nature of Reiki, and I hope this will cause offence to no one.

I have also made some references to Reiki Guides. I don't usually mention Guides in my Reiki I class. But by the time students are ready to learn Reiki II they have started to realize that Reiki has a tangible spiritual element. Some people consider they are just feeling the Ki, the energy, but others believe that there are higher vibrational beings that want to assist us in working with Reiki. It doesn't matter what you believe it is, but do know that you can communicate with it through your intention, that you can call on it to assist you in healing and indeed in all things. Above all, don't be afraid of it. If you prefer not to work with this aspect of Reiki, simply decide not to and you will not know that it is there.

I have also used the titles 'patient' and 'recipient' interchangeably to describe the person receiving Reiki from you. However, I have very specifically used the title 'client' to represent those that are paying you for Reiki as part of a professional relationship.

I had always assumed that I would include drawings of the Reiki II symbols in this book. However, as the time came to include them, I found myself being reminded of the very basic premise that the Reiki symbols are to be kept secret, known only to those who have studied the appropriate level of Reiki. Whilst the symbols are now in the public domain I strongly felt that I needed to honour the commitment I made when I was attuned to keep them secret. I know other authors have chosen to include the symbols, particularly so that errors in drawing could be corrected. However, I have made it clear that this book is not intended to replace a Reiki class, but to enhance it. On that basis, the symbols that you will be taught by your Reiki Master are the symbols that you will be attuned to and the symbols that you should use, even if they are different from those that I teach. On this basis there seemed to be no value in my including the symbols in this book.

I cannot stress how important it is to simply start using Reiki. It is important to use it on others but it is even more important to use it on yourself. Therefore I encourage you to dictate any of the exercises and hand positions into a recorder for your own personal use or for use with recipients.

Reiki Blessings,
Jacq

1

HOW TO USE THIS BOOK

This book is not intended to be a substitute for attending a Reiki class. Reiki Master Teachers may use this book to support teaching. Alternatively, it can be used by a student, either as preparation for attending a class or as revision and support after taking a class.

There is no set syllabus in the teaching of Reiki and no regulation in the way that Reiki is taught, at least in the UK. There is much more content that could be taught at both first and second levels than there is time for teaching, so it is hoped that this manual will help you to fill in any gaps in your learning and/or teaching.

Choosing a style of Reiki, a Reiki Master Teacher and a Reiki class are usually interconnected, as the majority of Reiki Masters will specialize in only one or two styles of Reiki, and will teach either online or face to face and not both. Don't be overwhelmed by the choices available; what is most important is to get started on your Reiki journey. If you are feeling brave just follow your gut instinct – I firmly believe that Reiki will lead you to the class that is exactly right for you. However, here are some thoughts to bear in mind.

CHOOSING A STYLE OF REIKI

There are an increasing number of styles of Reiki. In part due to the history and the separate development of Reiki in the West and in Japan (for more on this, read Chapter 3, The History of Reiki), there is some confusion over exactly what is meant by the term 'traditional' Reiki.

There are people who believe that, as Reiki is a Japanese technique, it is best to learn it in the way that its founder, Sensei Mikao Usui, taught it, in which case learning the Japanese style of Reiki is probably the most similar. However there are significant differences in culture between the West and Japan, and we each have our own learning styles.

Sensei Usui taught his students employing methods used in martial arts training, with weekly classes, homework to complete between classes, and each student progressing through the levels at the pace that matched their spiritual development. Students would take at least a year to reach the first level, several years to reach the second level, and very few students ever reached the highest level. Classes taught in the Japanese style will usually follow the Japanese levels of Shoden, Okuden and Shinpiden, rather than the Western Reiki levels of I, II and Master.

Some looking to learn the 'traditional' method of Reiki in fact mean the traditional *Western* style of teaching as taught by Mrs Takata, and probably styled 'Usui Reiki', although this phrase is often used more broadly. Many of the changes in curriculum and style of teaching made by Mrs Takata made the training much more suitable to a student from the West. For example, Western-style Reiki classes are usually taught over a single, or at most two, days per level for each of Reiki I and II. There is no set curriculum for this style of Reiki, although core elements will usually include teaching what Reiki is, the Reiki Principles and how to give a Reiki healing both to yourself and to others using a set of standard hand positions. It is essential that the class includes an attunement.

There are many other styles of Reiki, and more are being channelled all the time. Some are intended as follow-on or more advanced forms of Reiki, such as Karuna™ Reiki and Raku Kei Reiki, and some of which are standalone, such as Angelic Reiki or Seichem.

Unless you have an interest in a particular style of Reiki, I recommend you start with a form of Usui Reiki. This is by far the most commonly taught style in the West, and what I teach the majority of the time. It will give you good instruction in the basics, enabling you to experience using Reiki immediately. You can progress to a more advanced style if and when you are ready.

Not all styles of Reiki are approved by The Reiki Council, so if you think that you may one day like to practice in the UK as a registered Reiki practitioner or even go on to be a Master Teacher, be sure to check the acceptability of a particular style on The Reiki Council website.

CHOOSING A REIKI CLASS

You will find Reiki being offered as both face-to-face classes and online. There is much debate between Reiki Master Teachers as to whether an online attunement is effective in passing Reiki from Master to student. Although I only teach face to face, during the pandemic lockdown in 2020 I came across a number of prospective students who had a great and immediate need of Reiki. I taught these students the basics and gave them attunements over video calls, and I am satisfied that the attunements did work. However, the teaching was given on the understanding that students would attend a face-to-face class once lockdown was over and I am again only teaching face to face.

Although it is possible to learn Reiki online, you need to make sure that you will have ongoing support from your Master, that you understand how to carry out a Reiki healing and that you have had plenty of time to practise giving healing to others. Also be aware that, at the time of writing, online courses do not meet the requirements of The Reiki Council for registration as a Reiki practitioner in the UK.

Classes can be taught in a single day or over a weekend or even over a series of evenings. A face-to-face class will give you the luxury of spending time with people of like mind, and I often find my students exchanging contact details at the end of the day. Ideally, at both Reiki I and Reiki II level you should be looking for at least seven hours of teaching content, and this teaching content should be divided between teaching theory and allowing lots of time for practice. A small class size will give the opportunity for more individual attention and to interact more, whereas a larger class size gives more opportunity to meet others with different skills and experiences. Learning on a one-to-one basis makes it impossible to learn the hand positions, as it is necessary for the student to have someone to practise on other than the teacher. My preference is to teach classes of between five to eight people.

Aside from the practicalities, Reiki classes should be fun, the teaching should be open and inclusive, and you should have the opportunity to ask any questions that you have. Don't be afraid to contribute to the class. If you have a burning desire to share something I can promise you that there will be someone in the class who needs to hear it!

CHOOSING A REIKI MASTER

To be qualified to teach, a person must attain the Reiki Master Teacher level, not to be confused with the optional Reiki Master Practitioner level, which is not a teaching qualification. If you are interested, you can ask to see a copy of their lineage, which should show their Reiki 'family tree' tracing all the way back to Mikao Usui.

Reiki Masters come from all walks of life and all backgrounds. Some may be very logical in their approach, others very spiritual. Either way, a Reiki Master should be kind and caring and interested in their students' development. Try to find a Reiki Master who offers ongoing support, particularly through Reiki Shares or healing circles where you can practise your Reiki and meet socially outside of class.

Don't feel that you have to keep the same Master throughout your training; it can be very interesting and enlightening to experience the teaching of several different Reiki Masters, either by taking the same level several times, or by taking different levels with different Masters. You will see from my lineage that I have three Reiki Masters; one was very spiritual, one much more logical and the other a lovely combination of the two. They have each taught me valuable lessons, not just the basics of Reiki, but different ways to live a Reiki-focused life, and I love them all dearly.

WHAT TO WEAR

For Reiki classes at all levels comfortable clothing is appropriate. Trousers or leggings rather than a skirt may make it easier to climb on and off the treatment table. You may want to dress in layers as people often get hot when they're using Reiki, so it's nice to have a jumper or cardigan that you can slip off and on as necessary. Most of all wear something that makes you feel confident, something which, in the words of Marie Kondo, 'sparks joy'.

WHEN TO PROGRESS FROM REIKI I TO REIKI II

You may be tempted to book onto your Reiki II class at the same time as you book your Reiki I class, and some Reiki Masters teach Reiki I and II on consecutive days, perhaps over a weekend. However, the Ki takes time to build, and if you take too many levels too quickly it can be quite disorienting. Reiki also starts to make changes in your life following your first class, and it is easier to allow these changes to happen gradually, especially if you have other things going on in your life. Therefore, I recommend that you allow at least twenty-one days between classes; most commonly my students wait about three months. You will become aware when the Ki has stopped developing, and intuitively you will know when the time is right for you to move on to the next level.

Some students find that Reiki I is sufficient for their needs and never move on to Reiki II. Some move on several years after Reiki I. If you are at all uncertain, discuss this with your Reiki Master.

You may come across a third level of Reiki called 'Reiki IIIA', 'Advanced Reiki Training' or 'Reiki Master Practitioner'. This level was introduced by William Rand as a Master level for those that wanted to learn the Reiki Master symbol to use in healing, but had no interest in teaching. As well as learning the master symbol, this level usually includes a number of advanced healing methods and advice on running a Reiki practice. Generally, it is not necessary to have this level to work as a Reiki Practitioner (although certain employers may require it). This is also an optional level to take on the route to Reiki Master Teacher level. Again, if and when this level is right for you, you will find yourself drawn to the right class.

2

WHAT IS REIKI?

Reiki (pronounced ray – key) is a Japanese word, and it is most often translated as Universal Life-force Energy; 'Rei' meaning Universal, and 'Ki' meaning life-force energy. However, it is not as simple as you might think to find a satisfying direct translation of some Japanese words, especially one such as 'Reiki', which is an old word, and not in common usage today. The translation to Universal Life-force Energy is an over-simplification.

The Japanese characters that are put together to form words can take on different meanings or nuances when combined with other characters to form a single *kanji* (character). Added to this, many kanji also operate as pictographs, the image of the kanji giving as much information as to the meaning as the individual radicals. It is not unusual in Japan for a conversation to divert into a discussion of the meaning of a single kanji, even when the conversation is amongst adults!

So whilst 'Rei' most directly translates as 'universal', depending upon context it can also mean 'sacred', 'wisdom', 'divine essence' or 'mysterious power'. And 'ki'

The word 'Reiki' written in Japanese kanji.

when used generally most directly translates as 'life-force energy', but can also mean 'universal energy' or 'cosmic', and when used in referring to an individual can mean 'intention', 'mood' or 'character' (as in a person of good character). Most interesting of all, both 'Rei' and 'ki' can be translated in particular contexts as 'spirit' and 'soul'.

But perhaps rather than words, it is more important to understand the concept of Reiki. We use the word 'Reiki' today to describe both the healing system devised by Sensei Usui (and the subject of this book), and as the name of the energy used in this healing method. In the energetic sense, Reiki is both simply and profoundly the energy that surrounds, connects and is within every thing in the Universe; it is the force that, in 1944, Max Planck named the 'Divine Matrix'.

Reiki the energy is as old as time itself. You may already know it by other names such as *Prana* (India) or *Ch'i/Qi* (China). It is also the energy of quantum physics. It is in and around all things. All things are made of energy; all things are made of Ki.

'There is only one life force in the Universe.'[1]

Chuang-Tzu

In order to be healthy physically, mentally, emotionally, and spiritually, the Ki in and around our bodies needs to be clean, clear, vibrating at the appropriate level and constantly moving in and around our bodies and interacting with our surrounding environment. Many illnesses and diseases are caused by negative energy

The word 'Ch'i' or 'Ki' written in calligraphy.

or by energy blocks in the body and the aura. With a gentle laying on of hands, anyone with Reiki training can use Reiki to clean and clear the Ki, to remove any blockages, to restore the natural flow of Ki in and around the body and to adjust our energetic vibrations. Our physical bodies are then able to heal themselves. This ability of our bodies to self-heal is also enhanced by the state of relaxation that is induced by Reiki. Because Reiki enables the body to heal itself, Reiki can be used to heal all diseases at all levels; physical, mental and emotional.

Although Reiki is powerful, it works very gently, and so can be used in healing all people from babies to the very old. Nobody and nothing is too fragile to receive Reiki. You can also give Reiki to people who don't appear to be ill at all, just as an energy boost.

Reiki is spiritual in the sense that it is something that is greater than what we traditionally think of as our selves. But it is not religious, and using Reiki does not conflict with any religious or other belief system. Because Reiki is spiritual it can only be used to do good. Reiki cannot be used to do physical, mental or emotional harm; if you try to use it in this way it either won't work, or might even bounce back on you! It cannot be used to manipulate; it cannot even be used to make someone fall in love with you, unless that is to their highest good!

Whilst in the West Reiki is most commonly used for healing, Sensei Usui sought and taught the use of Reiki for spiritual growth, as it can aid in meditation and the discovery and fulfilment of one's life purpose. It can also be used in all areas of personal development; it assists in learning, goal setting and manifestation. In fact there isn't anything that doesn't benefit from the application of Reiki. The more you work with Reiki, the more you will find you are bringing your best self to everything that you do.

Interestingly, you don't need to believe in Reiki for it to work. A sceptical recipient does need to consent to receiving Reiki, as Reiki will not flow where it is not wanted. But it is enough to have an open mind, to agree simply to let Reiki in. In fact my first sceptical client is about to start training as a Reiki Master!

Although Sensei Usui named his system the 'Usui Reiki Ryoho' (Usui Reiki Healing Method), the word 'Reiki' is now used in common parlance as the name to describe the healing system that he devised. I occasionally meet people who consider themselves to have Reiki even though they haven't taken Reiki training. They are very possibly using Reiki (the energy) in healing. But they can only claim to be Reiki (the method) healers if they have been taught Reiki by a Reiki Master Teacher with a lineage that traces back to Mikao Usui, and have received the crucial initiation, which we call an attunement. This is not to say that any other energy healing method is less good, simply that it is not Reiki.

It is worth pointing out that I have a number of clients who are spiritual healers (not Reiki trained) who regularly come to me for healing. They find that a Reiki healing restores their energy levels. Those that go on to take Reiki training say that the Reiki energy feels different from the energy they were working with before. This doesn't challenge the view that Reiki is the energy that is all around us; just that Reiki comes in different vibrations, like ice-cream comes in different flavours.

Reiki is extremely versatile. Because it works with the body's own immune system it can be used to heal all things. It is a complementary therapy that can be used alongside other holistic therapies or allopathic (Western) medicine, speeding healing, reducing pain and often reducing the amount of drugs required (but this must always be decided by the recipient's doctor). There are no contra-indications to the use of Reiki. You might read elsewhere that Reiki shouldn't be used on a broken bone until it has been re-set, the concern being that Reiki might heal the bone out of alignment. Or that Reiki should not be used to hcal a severed finger or toe until it has been re-attached, the concern being that the nerve endings would seal over before they could be re-joined. But neither of these concerns are valid. Reiki is an intelligent energy, and used in these first-aid situations it can stop bleeding, ease pain and relieve shock.

Due to lack of funding, there is little science-based research into the effectiveness of Reiki. But there is a wealth of anecdotal evidence and personal experience of the benefits, both in healing and personal development. Once you start working with Reiki you won't be able to doubt that it is real. The movement of Ki is tangible to most people, who will sense it as heat, cold, tingling, prickling or swirling. What is more, some people can see Reiki, usually as a bright white or coloured light. One of my favourite things is the look on the face of a sceptical student when they feel Reiki for the first time!

THE ATTUNEMENT

The reason that you cannot learn Reiki entirely from a book is because the gift of Reiki is passed from Master to student through the attunement process. We are all born with a supply of spiritual Ki. The attunement is a ritual that massively increases the amount of Ki present in the body, and effectively switches on the student's ability to channel Reiki, and to continually replenish their Ki.

The entire responsibility for the attunement is with the teacher. The student does not need to be concerned that they 'didn't do it right' or that Reiki won't work for them. Provided that the attunement process is followed with the appropriate intention, and the student consents to receiving Reiki, then the attunement will work.

Depending upon the style of Reiki being taken, each Reiki level has between one and four attunements. Once you have had the appropriate attunement(s) it will give you Reiki for life, and doesn't need to be renewed even if you don't use your Reiki often or at all. However, many Reiki Masters will give you a top-up Reiki attunement if you desire, and this will make your use of and sensitivity to Reiki stronger.

Your attunement should be a very enjoyable experience, so please don't worry about what you may or may not experience, as whatever you experience will be exactly right for you. The attunement comprises a number of stages: first the student is placed inside appropriate energetic protection, and then the chakras are opened. Reiki is then invited in through the crown chakra and is placed specifically in the head and hands of the student. Finally Reiki is invited into the body, is anchored into the root chakra and empowers each of the chakras. Often an appropriate affirmation or 'prayer' is planted into the root chakra by the Reiki Master Teacher.

Whilst an attunement can be carried out anywhere, and can take as little as five minutes, usually the process is carried out in a pleasant environment and as part of a guided meditation. Done this way it can take up to thirty minutes, especially if a number of students are being attuned at the same time. Where and how the attunement is performed might be one factor that you take into account when you select a Reiki class.

The range of possible reactions to the attunement is wide, but most importantly whatever you experience will be exactly right for you. The attunement will have worked – even if you don't really feel anything! At the very least, you will hopefully feel deeply relaxed and have a sense of incredible calm. Reactions can include seeing colours or a bright light, hearing music, seeing angelic visions, feeling Ki moving around your body and experiencing deep emotions. I even once attuned a student who saw a dragon!

Usually after the attunement there is some time to make notes and to discuss your experience.

Some time after the attunement you will start to feel Reiki in your hands. The sensation may start during the attunement, or more likely will start later in the day. For some people it can take up to three days for the sensations to be apparent. The sensations can be of heat or cold, a glowing, tingling or even pins and needles, and will steadily increase, especially when you start to give Reiki to someone else. In the first few weeks and months after your attunement, you may notice that your Reiki switches on sporadically. In time, you will easily control your Reiki by thinking 'Reiki on', and if you wish, although not strictly necessary, 'Reiki off'.

If, in the very rare case that even after some time has passed, after you have given yourself several self-healings and after you have given a Reiki healing to at least one other person, you still do not feel Reiki in your hands, and are not noticing any effects of Reiki, do contact your Reiki Master who will be able to re-attune you.

LINEAGE

Once you have received an attunement you will have a Reiki lineage. This is your place in the family tree that links us all back to Sensei Usui. Your lineage will change to that of your new Reiki Master if you take a higher level with a different Master, until you are yourself a Reiki Master Teacher. Then the Master that first taught you the Reiki Master Teacher level will always be your lineage, no matter what you do after that.

This is my Western Reiki lineage:

Sensei Mikao Usui
Chajiro Hayashi
Mrs Takata
Iris Ishikuro
Diane McCumber
William Rand
Allan Sweeney
Tina Reibl
Jacqueline Raison
My students

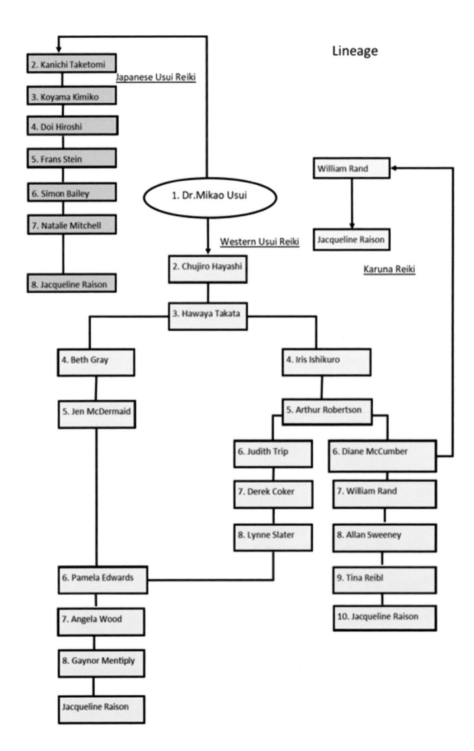

Lineage

Author's lineage for Usui Western, Japanese and Karuna™ Reiki.

THE TWENTY-ONE-DAY CLEARING PROCESS

Following each attunement, it takes twenty-one days for the increased Ki in your body to cycle through your chakras, starting with the root chakra the day after your attunement and the sacral the next day. It will continue to move through the chakras in turn for the rest of that week, returning back to the root chakra for the start of the second week and finally again for the start of the third week. The clearing process ends with the crown chakra twenty-one days after the attunement.

During this period it is essential you give yourself a Reiki healing every day. After a Reiki I attunement the self-healing should be ten to fifteen minutes each day; after Reiki II, twenty to thirty minutes each day. In the first couple of days after the attunement you might notice some detox-type symptoms, such as minor aches and pains; you might feel very emotional, especially after the Reiki II attunement. But you will also start to become aware of Reiki in your hands every time you think of it.

During this time Reiki will be getting stronger. You will start to notice little changes in your life generally. You might find yourself smiling more, feeling a little happier. You may suddenly come across new people with similar interests to yours. You may start to appreciate nature, peace and quiet, and simply spending time in your own company more than you did before. You may find that you are leaving behind bad habits and negative thought patterns that no longer serve you. You may start noticing more in life to be grateful for. If there are things that you have perhaps been struggling with for some time, you may be surprised at how easily they now start to resolve.

You might like to take the opportunity to use this twenty-one-day clearing period as a body, mind and spirit 'detox'. If you would like to do this there are many programmes you could follow, but basically try to: drink six to eight glasses of water a day; cut out flour, sugar and processed foods and follow a healthy eating programme; avoid newspapers and other negative influences; avoid noise and crowds; do a little light exercise and spend a little time each day in nature.

THE REIKI PRECEPTS

There are two rules, which I call the Reiki Precepts, that you must follow whenever you are giving Reiki:

1. You must not give Reiki to someone without their consent; and

2. You should obtain an exchange of value for giving Reiki.

Consent

Consent can only be given by someone who understands what they are consenting to; they also need to be able to communicate that consent to you. Make sure you can explain what Reiki is in language that the patient can understand. As you start working with family and friends you will know what language to use to explain it to them, based on that person's age and background (for example, consider how you would explain Reiki to a three-year-old, a seven-year-old or an elderly parent).

In most situations your patient will have asked you for Reiki, or you will have offered it and they will have accepted, so it is easy to know that you have consent.

When you are giving Reiki as a practitioner (after you have taken Reiki II) your client will have booked an appointment, you will discuss the treatment beforehand and the client will give you a signed consent form. You can treat this as sufficient consent.

However, you will come across people who are in need of healing but who either cannot understand what Reiki is, or cannot communicate their consent to you; for example a baby, a dementia sufferer, or someone in a coma. In Western medicine in such circumstances hospitals will accept the consent of a next of kin. In truth this is highly inadequate. We rarely discuss these things with others in sufficient detail, and our next of kin will be influenced by their own needs and fears. In Western medicine a Living Will or 'do not resuscitate' form can be used. But it really is impossible even for ourselves to imagine what treatment we would want in any number of different circumstances at some time in the future. However one of the many wonders of Reiki is that we can connect directly with the subconscious of the patient to ask for their consent, regardless of their ability to communicate at a conscious level.

There are two ways of doing this:

Intuitive consent – quieten your mind, and concentrate on what you are asking. In your mind silently ask the patient if they would like to receive a Reiki healing. You will usually receive a very clear indication in your head as to whether or not they want Reiki. Don't over-think this – your first thought is usually the right answer.

However, if you are afraid that you will not know if what you hear in your head is the truth or simply what you want to hear, then try this second method.

Offer Reiki – hold in your mind the offer of sending Reiki if they would like it. Turn your hands palm upwards, and think 'Reiki on'. If they consent you will feel the Reiki start to flow, if they don't then it won't. I use this second method whenever I am offering Reiki to animals.

Value

If you are Reiki II or over, and have appropriate insurance, then you can charge for giving Reiki, which is a clear exchange of value. But otherwise you will need to find another way of getting value in exchange. For example you might exchange a Reiki healing for:

- A healing in return.
- A skill exchange.
- Lunch or a cup of coffee.
- Jobs around the house (especially good for kids!).

There are some situations where you may feel you are already in debt, for example when offering healing to a loving parent, a baby or pet, and this is perfectly fine. This rule is not so absolute as the rule on consent. However, if you ever find that your Reiki isn't flowing as strongly as usual, just check that there has been an appropriate exchange of value.

THE REIKI PRINCIPLES

The Reiki Principles

Just for today, I will not worry;
Just for today, I will not anger;
Just for today, I will give thanks for my many blessings;

Just for today, I will do my work honestly;
Just for today, I will show kindness to all living things.

Although knowledge of the Reiki Principles is not necessary to be a healer, nevertheless they are core to the Reiki system, and in being attuned to Reiki you are confirming your acceptance of the Reiki Principles. The principles were not written by Sensei Usui; they are tenets of ancient wisdom that were used in Tendai Buddhism by the Shugendo sect as long ago as the ninth century. They were popularized in Usui's time by the then Emperor Mutsuhito. Sensei Usui incorporated the Principles into his Reiki system, writing that these Principles are 'The secret art of inviting happiness, the miraculous medicine of all diseases'; and so by living by these principles we, as healers, begin to heal ourselves.

Just for Today...

Each of the Principles begins with the phrase 'Just for today...' This makes our goal of following the principles more manageable; dividing a seemingly unachievable lifetime task into many smaller attainable daily goals. There is a reason why 'Just for today...' is used by both Alcoholics Anonymous and UK Narcotics Anonymous. New Year resolutions rarely work, because a commitment to do, or to stop doing, something forever is just not realistic. More manageable commitments, such as thirty-day boot camps and dry January, often do work simply because they seem more achievable. The same applies with the Reiki Principles. If we only have to commit that we will not get angry *today*, that is easier than thinking we can never get angry again.

Beyond that though, 'just for today' reminds us to live in the moment. That in fact this moment is all we have. Yesterday is gone; tomorrow may never come. All that we can ever have is this present moment. If we use our time today to dwell on what happened in the past, or to be concerned about what may happen in the future then we do not make the best of today. It is only by living the best day today that we can discover our best selves and live our best lives.

I Will not Worry

By definition you can only worry about a future event. Even if you are worrying about something that happened in the past, your worry is the impact that it will have upon your future, and so if we worry, we are not living in the present.

When our minds think about something, our bodies don't know that the thing is just imagined; it behaves as if what is being thought about is really happening. If you need convincing about this, just spend a moment right now imagining that you are eating a lemon. Imagine the smell, the feel of it in your hands, perhaps taking a knife and cutting it in half. Then finally biting into it. Take a moment, put the book down, and try it now... You will notice that your mouth waters. Your body is preparing itself to eat the lemon – it doesn't know that you are only imagining the lemon. It is just the same with anything we think about – the body cannot differentiate between something that is real and something that is only imagined. When we worry about something, it is not so obvious as the mouth watering in the lemon example, but our bodies are preparing to deal with whatever it is we are worrying about in just the same way; and so it will produce

adrenaline and cortisol, preparing you for 'fight or flight'. It is not healthy for us to live in a constant state of alert.[2] They say that 85 per cent of what we worry about never actually happens. So, we are filling our bodies with stress hormones worrying about something that very likely won't happen.

> 'My life has been filled with terrible misfortune; most of which never happened.'
>
> *Michel de Montaigne*

The Law of Attraction states that if we think about positive things we will attract positive things, and if we think about negative things we will attract negative things. In other words at an energetic level, like attracts like. When we are happy and in a high vibrational state we attract good and positive things. When we are afraid and in a low vibrational state we attract negative and unpleasant things. Worry is a low vibration negative emotion. So in all likelihood, if we are a great worrier we become a great manifestor of exactly what we are worrying about!

I Will not Anger

Most of us already understand that anger is a negative emotion. We talk about being 'eaten up by anger'; in anger we often lash out, verbally if not physically. We can experience an almost complete loss of control. Anger, especially when it is held on to or repressed, is bad for our health contributing to heart disease, stroke, loss of lung function and suppression of our immune system.

But we live in a world where we are surrounded by things that, quite frankly, it is reasonable to get angry about. Anger is said to be a secondary emotion – a defensive reaction to fear, grief or sadness or recognition of a lack of control, and is almost always aimed at someone else. Because of this, when we are angry we usually don't take responsibility for what has made us angry, and therefore we don't believe that we own the resolution. This isn't true, and we always do own the resolution. Not that we individually 'own' world hunger (although collectively we certainly do!), but we must each find our own way of making peace with whatever it is that makes us angry. Whether that is donating to a relevant charity or getting on a plane and going to do something about it.

Perhaps you might like to think of this principle more as 'I will not hold onto anger'. Use a flare up of righteous anger to spur you into action to resolve the thing that is making you angry – either by solving it if you can, or if you can't by finding the way that you can continue to live with it, and take back control.

I Will Give Thanks for my Many Blessings

Going back to the thought that like attracts like, or Bob Proctor's 'What you think about, you bring about', gratitude is one of the highest vibrational states, and when you take time to be grateful for who you are and what you have, you get more of the things that you are grateful for.

If you are open to starting a gratitude practice, I recommend that you find something that fits in easily with your daily life. If you already have a gratitude practice, try and extend it a little. You need to try to get to a place where you are in the vibration of gratitude more than half the time. So if you already list things you are grateful for each day, extend this practice by writing not only what you are grateful for, but *why* you are grateful for each item. If you are looking for new ways to work with gratitude I highly recommend Rhonda Byrne's twenty-eight-day gratitude practice in her book *The Secret*.[3]

(Simon & Schuster UK, 2006).

'What you think, you become.
What you feel, you attract.
What you imagine, you create.'

Gautama Buddha

Ideas for a Gratitude Practice

- Every day write a list of three, five or even ten things that you are grateful for.

- Last thing at night, go over all that happened in the day and identify the things that you were most grateful for.

- Whenever you notice something happening that you are grateful for, stop for a moment, really concentrate on how it makes you feel, and then in your mind, say thank you three times. Do this to show appreciation:

- For everything you eat and drink.

- For the people who are closest to you.

- For the weather, nature, birdsong and trees.

- For your body and all it can do.

- In business every time you receive an order or payment.

- If you have a family, spend time together sharing the things that happened that day that you are grateful for, perhaps over a meal.

I Will do my Work Honestly

This principle goes beyond a commitment not to steal paper clips from the office! Nor is it necessarily about the nine-to-five office job that most of us have or have had. Remember that Sensei Usui didn't always have that kind of job.

Your work in this context is what you spend most of your time doing. If we expand the word 'honestly' to 'with integrity', we are getting closer to the meaning of this principle – whatever it is that you do with your time, do it with integrity. If something is worth your time, do it properly. Very often when we do things, we are not doing them with our whole intention and focus. Our mind is somewhere else, thinking about other things that we feel we ought to be doing, or would prefer to be doing. Thich Nhat Hanh, influential Zen Buddhist monk and peace campaigner, said, 'Wash the dishes to wash the dishes'. In other words, don't wash the dishes to clean up the kitchen or as part of any other purpose. If it is worth your time to wash the dishes, then wash the dishes. Be alive to whatever you are doing in that moment. We women particularly pride ourselves on an ability to 'multi-task', but we know in our heart of hearts that when we do this, far from doing our work honestly, in fact we don't do any one part of it very well at all.

And know also that the most important thing we can work on is ourselves. Taking your first Reiki class will be a step in this direction!

I Will Show Kindness to all Living Things

When I discuss this principle with students in class it seems to be a continuum along which we are all moving in the same direction, but at different rates. At the start of the continuum are those who are managing to put spiders out of the house instead of killing them, but perhaps would still call pest control in to get a wasps' nest removed. Some wouldn't eat veal and ensure that they buy free range, whilst some are choosing to be vegetarian or even vegan. If you are a pet-lover and think you have no challenge from this principle, what about ticks and fleas or horse flies? You are showing kindness to your pet by killing ticks and fleas, but are you being kind to the ticks and fleas?

There is no judgement here; there is no judgement with Reiki. Just a commitment to keep an awareness that none of us are perfect, and to keep moving along

the continuum in the right direction. I do give my pets flea tablets, I would put a mouse trap down, and I would have a wasps' nest removed if necessary; but where I can, I give three days' notice (communicated through Reiki) to warn the animal to leave first. As you continue to work with this principle you will find it becomes easier, as any *irrational* fears of animals will disappear, making it easier to live alongside them.

Even if you still believe that you have nothing more to learn from this principle, I will take this opportunity to remind you that you, too, are a living thing, and that perhaps the greatest challenge of this principle is to be kind to yourself.

Working with the Reiki Principles

There is tremendous value to be gained in working with the Reiki Principles on a daily basis. There are many ways in which you can do this:

- Carry a card with the principles on it in your wallet or somewhere that you will see it often.

- Recite the principles as soon as you wake up.

- Recite the Reiki Principles at the end of your daily self-healing (perhaps three times).

- Recite the principles before you fall asleep.

- Meditate on a principle for a day.

- Meditate on a principle every day for a week.

- Recite the appropriate principle when you realize you are not following it.

- When you realize you are worrying or angry, try reciting 'I now let go of my worry/anger' until you have raised your vibration.

THE HISTORY OF REIKI

MRS TAKATA'S STORY

*Mikao Usui, the founder of
Usui Reiki Ryoho.*

Dr Mikao Usui was a teacher in a Christian school in Kyoto, Japan. One day when he was teaching a class of children, they asked him if he believed that Jesus healed the sick in the way that the Bible said he did. He confirmed that he did believe it. They then asked him how Jesus healed.

When he realized that he didn't really know the answer to the children's question, rather than give them an inadequate answer he took up a quest that would take him seven years to complete and would take him halfway around the world.

He started by doing a degree in Philosophy and Religion at the University of Chicago. When this didn't get him any closer to his answer, he travelled to India to learn about healing in Buddhism. The Buddhist monks told him that they couldn't understand his obsession with physical healing, and insisted that healing began in the mind. Again, he was no closer to learning how Jesus healed.

However, he did learn about the existence of some ancient scrolls that were kept in a temple in Tibet. The scrolls were written in the ancient Indian Sanskrit language, and so he set about learning the language and then travelled to Tibet to read them.

It was in these scrolls that Dr Usui found the healing symbols that concentrate and amplify healing energy and form the basis of Reiki. However, even then Usui had no idea how to use all that he had learned as a method to heal in the way that Jesus healed.

Usui felt that he had failed in his mission, and he returned to his home city of Kyoto. He decided to spend time fasting and in meditation in the hope that this would bring the answer he was looking for. He travelled to Mount Kurama, a very spiritual place to the north-east of Kyoto. He climbed the mountain, passing many temples and shrines, with only a goatskin of water. He collected twenty-one pebbles and sat down amidst the tree roots to meditate.

At the end of each day he discarded one of the pebbles, and so he spent twenty-one days fasting and meditating. On the final day, he had a vision of the symbols that he had discovered in the Tibetan temple coming to him in bright lights. Through this enlightenment Sensei Usui learned how to heal using the system we now know as Reiki.

On descending from Mount Kurama, Usui experienced the power of Reiki almost immediately. He stubbed his toe during the descent and it was bleeding. He held his toe in his hand, and within a minute the bleeding stopped. At the bottom of the mountain Usui found a café and ordered a full breakfast. As it

Trees where Sensei Usui meditated on Mount Kurama.

was obvious from the length of his beard that he had been fasting for some time, the café owner wanted to serve him a simple broth, but Usui insisted on and ate the full breakfast without any indigestion. The cook's daughter, who delivered his meal, was crying with toothache. Dr Usui laid on his hand against her cheek, gave the girl Reiki, and the toothache stopped almost immediately.

He demonstrated his healing gift on a local priest. They decided that he should immediately start healing the beggars on the street, and that once he had done so the priest would find employment for them. After healing in the slums of Kyoto Dr Usui then travelled, taking his healing more widely through Japan. He was devastated to find on his return several years later that many people had not accepted the healing he had given and were living just as they were before. They did not appreciate being healed – they did not want changes in their lives. They placed the same value on his healing gift as they had paid for it... nothing.

Deeply upset, he returned to the monastery to meditate on his failure to provide a permanent cure. During his meditation he was reminded of what the Buddhist monks had said to him years ago – that healing begins in the mind.

As a result of what he learned in meditation, he decided to incorporate into his teaching two Reiki precepts, concerning consent and value, to govern to whom Reiki healing is given; and the five Reiki Principles to aid in the development of Reiki students.

Mrs Takata went on to tell us that Dr Usui did little to pass on the healing skills he had learned. She did tell us that Usui trained one student, a doctor in the Japanese navy, Dr Chujiro Hayashi. She told us that Dr Hayashi set up a Reiki clinic in Japan where he offered Reiki healing and training, and that he trained fifteen Reiki Masters, only one of whom was not Japanese. This was Mrs Takata herself, a native of Hawaii, who had been healed of serious illnesses (a tumour, gallstones, asthma and appendicitis have been mentioned) at the clinic. Dr Hayashi was reluctant to teach a non-Japanese student, but Mrs Takata refused to leave the clinic until he finally relented and taught her Reiki I. It was a

Mrs Takata.

condition of the training that she stay and work in the clinic for a year, which she did, and at the end of the year she was trained to Reiki level II.

As World War II approached, Dr Hayashi attuned Mrs Takata to the Master level, allowing her to start teaching Reiki, which she did throughout Hawaii, USA and Canada. At the outbreak of the war Dr Hayashi, knowing that he would be re-called to serve in the Japanese Navy, chose instead to take his own life. Some time later, Mrs Takata reported that Hayashi-san's clinic in Tokyo was bombed, killing all the remaining Reiki Masters in Japan, and leaving Mrs Takata as the sole remaining Reiki teacher in the world.

THE TRUE HISTORY

We now know that the history as told by Mrs Takata is more of a parable or teaching story than a true history.

Mikao Usui was a Tendai Buddhist born in 1865. As a child he studied at a monastery near Mount Kurama. He studied martial arts from the age of twelve, and reached an extremely high level of proficiency. Usui was an academic who studied religion (including Zen Buddhism), numerology, psychology, and Chinese and Western medicine. Although both Chujiro Hayashi and Mrs Takata referred to him as Doctor, there is no evidence that Usui gained a doctorate whether in medicine or any other discipline.

Usui came of age during the reign of the Meiji Emperor Mutsuhito, as Japan was entering an age of rapid development, having re-opened to the West only about thirty years earlier. There was a collective movement towards wanting to protect Japanese traditions in the face of the new developments, and many spiritual and semi-spiritual practices were being developed along traditional Japanese lines at that time, including Aikido and Judo.

Like many others in Japan, Usui was seeking personal spiritual enlightenment, and he devised a method for doing so using concepts taken from Tendai Buddhism, Shintoism and martial arts. The principles that are referred to as the five Reiki Principles were actually used by a Tendai sect of Shugendo in the ninth century.

In Japan, methods such as these were usually kept within families for their own benefit. But Usui wanted to share his method. So it is true that Usui was a teacher, but he didn't teach children in a school, and he wasn't teaching healing. Rather, he taught spiritually minded individuals who were on the same journey towards enlightenment as he had been. He said that Usui Reiki was a method for achieving personal perfection. He would set his students methods to work on week by week, give them Reiju empowerments (Reiki blessings), check their journals and answer any questions. The method included Waka poetry, meditations and the Reiki Principles. He taught a large number of students, maybe 2,000 or more, and he created twenty Reiki Masters.

Waka Poetry

Waka, literally 'Japanese Poem' or 'Japanese Song', is a form of poetry that has been written in Japan for thousands of years. Emperor Meiji, Emperor of Japan during Mikao Usui's lifetime, wrote 125 Waka poems in ancient Japanese, mostly on the subjects of nature and relationships. When written in Japanese, the most common form of Waka poetry has only three lines, consisting of five, seven and five syllables respectively. Unfortunately this pattern is not usually preserved in the translation.

Sensei Usui used these Waka in his spiritual teaching.[4]

The Spirit

Whatever happens
In any situation
It is my wish that
The spirit remains
Without boundaries

In 1922 Usui started a clinic in Harajuku, Tokyo and launched the Usui Reiki Ryoho Gakkai (the Usui Reiki Healing Method Society).

Dr Chujiro Hayashi.

In 1923 there was a massive earthquake in Japan about fifty miles from Tokyo, and many people were severely injured in the resultant fires. Usui worked tirelessly healing the wounded. It was said that 'he cured and saved innumerable people... he extended hands of love over those who were suffering'.[5] He was granted an honorary title for his work (perhaps the source of the title 'Dr'). It was here that he met Dr Chujiro Hayashi and came to the attention of the imperial military. They wanted him to train the naval doctors in his method of healing. Usui knew that they would not be able to use the same method he had been teaching previously, as these men were not at all spiritual. Instead, in teaching them he incorporated ancient sacred symbols to introduce the energies that his traditional students took years to develop, devised the method of passing Reiki by attunement (known as Reiju in Japan). He also taught a number of techniques such as gassho, byosen scanning and Reiji-ho which are still taught and used in the Japanese style of Reiki today.

Usui urged Dr Hayashi (who had joined the Usui Reiki Ryoho Gakkai) to open a Reiki clinic and school in Tokyo, which he did. In or about 1936, some ten years after Usui's death, Mrs Takata, as we are told in her story, arrived at the clinic for healing.

After Usui's death, Dr Hayashi left the Usui Reiki Ryoho Gakkai, but the society was continued by Ushida-san, another Reiki Master trained by Usui. Contrary to what we were told by Mrs Takata, the society continues today, although its membership is ageing and declining. Very interestingly, Reiki is not well known in Japan. When students come to Japan to join one of my retreats I warn them not to tell the local Japanese people that they have come to learn Reiki, as they will get some very strange looks! This is because although Reiki has continued in Japan, it has continued in private, and not in public. Hayashi's clinic in Tokyo was continued after his death by his wife, but after she retired it closed. The few Reiki Masters still alive in Japan after the war have kept Reiki very secret; only a very few senior doctors and others of high status are invited to learn Reiki in Japan.

THE GROWTH OF REIKI IN THE WEST

Conversely, in the West there are now millions of people using Reiki. The credit for this must go to Dr Hayashi and Mrs Takata.

Although Hayashi only studied with Usui for a short time, he carried on Usui's work of developing the Reiki method to make it more accessible to the less spiritually minded. He added a number of standard hand positions for certain diseases and significantly reduced the time taken to teach Reiki by the development of the Reiju Reiki blessing – similar to the attunement process we now use.

Mrs Takata returned to Hawaii following her treatment and her Reiki training, and some six months later Dr Hayashi and his daughter visited her to help with the spread of Reiki through Hawaii. In 1938 Hayashi gave Mrs Takata her Reiki Master level, allowing her to teach. He did then return to Japan and take his own life.

Despite charging £10,000 (then the cost of a small house!) for Reiki Master training, Mrs Takata taught twenty-two Reiki Masters. She introduced further simplifications to the method, creating a set of eight standard hand positions to be used on the patient's front, which could be used in all treatments regardless of the disease complained of; and also an optional four hand positions that could be used on the back if desired. She also hugely simplified the teaching of Reiki. Hers is without doubt the most widely taught method of Reiki today, and therefore we must accept that her changes have been hugely successful.

THE TEACHING STORY

So why do we have these conflicting accounts of the Reiki history? Why would Mrs Takata create a story that has now been shown not to be true?

Mrs Takata was given her Reiki Master attunement in 1938, with a large part of the world on the brink of war. In 1940 Japan joined the Axis alliance, joining with Germany and Italy against Great Britain, and on 7 December 1941 they bombed Pearl Harbour, Hawaii. With the USA joining the war as a consequence, this would not have been a time for touting a Japanese healing system around the USA and Canada!

I believe that Mrs Takata introduced a number of elements to her story that made Reiki more palatable to the West at that time. For example, that Sensei Usui was teaching in a Christian school, when we know he was a Buddhist; and that he studied at the University of Chicago, which is simply not true.

Mrs Takata also created a beautiful story that is a joy to re-tell, and which feels very much in the spirit of Reiki. The story that she told can be seen as a parable or a teaching story, as it has a number of elements that subliminally introduce concepts that are important in the learning of Reiki:

■ Mrs Takata tells of a long journey in search of the truth. Although it is possible now to learn Reiki in a day, nevertheless this one day will likely be the start of a journey for you as well. Whilst the attunement introduces energies that would have taken Sensei Usui's students months if not years to experience, even after the accelerated learning of Western Reiki, working with Reiki is a path of continual learning.

■ She tells of setbacks encountered along the way; people that didn't appreciate the healing that they had received, causing self-doubt and a need to re-think. There is no doubt that a life with Reiki will be much smoother and more enjoyable than a life without Reiki. But having Reiki doesn't mean that you never get another headache, or that you never receive another bill that you can't pay, or that every patient will receive the healing that you would like for them. For Sensei Usui these setbacks led to greater learning, such as the importance of the Reiki Principles. Perhaps we can try to see the silver lining of each of our setbacks.

■ She tells of obstacles that needed to be circumvented. It is unlikely that we will need to learn a new language in the way that Sensei Usui had to learn Sanskrit in order to read the scrolls. But we may need to learn complementary skills such as the art of communication, first aid and how to run our own business.

- She tells us that Sensei Usui collected twenty-one pebbles, and that he threw away a pebble a day to keep track of time. If the purpose was purely to keep track of time, he could have collected a pebble a day, or carved a notch in a tree. But the significance of throwing a pebble away is to show us that there may be things in our lives now, perhaps unhealthy practices or limiting beliefs, that we will need to leave behind to enable us to grow.

- She shows us that healing cannot be given to those who do not want it, and that Reiki won't heal those that do not value it.

- She shows us that although Reiki is not a religion, and doesn't associate with any particular religion, it is spiritual and it is profound.

4

THE AURA AND CHAKRAS

The Aura

When we look at each other, most of us see our regular, physical bodies. But throughout time some clairvoyants and psychics have been able to see, or have otherwise been aware, that humans, animals, plants and crystals have an energy field that extends beyond the physical body.

The Indian spiritual tradition used the word *Prana* (in Sanskrit, literally 'life force') to describe a vital energy that they believed originated from the sun, flowed throughout the body and connected the body to all the elements. Some 3,000 years BCE the Chinese spiritual tradition used the word *Ch'i* (or *Qi*) when referring to a vapour-like vital life force comprising yin and yang, which was thought not only to be an integral part of, but to connect, all living things. In both traditions, it was recognized that it was necessary to keep this energy moving and balanced in order to be healthy. In both the Old and New Testaments of the Christian Bible, there are many references to light, fire, brightness or rainbows surrounding a holy figure. From the fourth century through to the Renaissance, we see the representation of this aura as halos or radiant light in religious art.

Discussions of the possibility of an energetic field surrounding living things slowly moved from the realms of religion to those of science. Chemist Baron von Reichenbach, whilst studying the impact of various substances on the human nervous system, proposed in 1839 the existence of an electro-magnetic force that surrounded most things. He called this the Odic Field. Modern scientists have so far failed to replicate his findings.

However as our understanding of physics has moved from the limitations of classical mechanics as founded by Newton to Einstein's theory of relativity, and as quantum theory becomes mainstream, I am confident that we are getting much closer to a scientific understanding of the aura and how energy healing works. For example, we now know that when two electrons vibrating together get separated, an 'invisible cord' forms between them, so that when they are

Were halos the artist's impression of an aura?

placed a distance apart when one is wiggled the other instantly knows (quantum entanglement).[6] We also now know that what we have previously thought of as solid is simply energy vibrating at a lower level.

These developments brought many scientists into the field of investigating energy. They began to measure this energy, using scientific methods to examine what it is made of, and they began to consider the relationship of this energy field to health and healing.

The word 'aura' was coined by Dr Walter Kilner to describe what he saw, using coloured screens and filters, as three distinct layers of 'mist' around the human body. A system called Radionics was developed by Drs de la Warr and Drown, which takes photographs of the energy field, identifying abnormalities in living tissue. A high-powered microscope has been used to observe pulsing energy named 'orgone' by psychiatrist Dr Wilhelm Reich.

So, although originally proposed by mystics, religionists and clairvoyants, advances in physics, particularly in the field of quantum mechanics, suggest it will not now be long before science is able to prove that all living things have an electromagnetic field which surrounds and envelopes them. What the aura is made of is less clear. It seems to have more substance than gas, but less than fluid; it may be made of many, many tiny particles. It is likely that the substance of the aura is something new that we haven't come across before. The

word 'bioplasma', first used by the Soviet Bioinformation Institute, is perhaps appropriate.

It is also clear that the aura acts as a kind of map that indicates what state our bodies are in. Disease can be caused by physical means (a broken leg), emotional means (heartbreak) or by mental means (paranoia). No matter the cause, disease will manifest in the aura before it manifests in the physical body. By learning to read and heal the aura we can heal physical, mental and emotional issues regardless of cause, and often before they manifest in the physical body.

Most clairvoyants agree that the aura has seven layers. The layers do not sit one on top of the other, as is often drawn. Rather, each outer layer overlaps the lower layers and all co-exist in the physical body. As each subsequent layer extends out a little further than the layer before, this gives the appearance of separate layers. The form of these layers alternates between being quite structured (the first, third, fifth and seventh layers) and being more fluid (the second, fourth and sixth layers). Each layer of the aura is associated with a different chakra and has a different purpose.

The first layer of the aura is a light blue or silver-grey, and follows the outline of the body, extending all around by an inch or two. This first layer relates to the physical body. We all existed as pure energy before we were born, and this layer of the aura is the blueprint and matrix upon which our physical body was created.

Any disease in the physical body is mapped on this layer of the aura.

The second layer of the aura is the emotional layer. It appears cloud-like, and can look light and misty or grey and heavy depending upon the emotional well-being of the person at the time. Some people can see various brilliant and vibrant colours in this layer. It overlays the physical body and the first layer, and extends beyond the first layer by an inch or two. Emotional issues can be healed in this layer of the aura. If they are not, they will work through the first layer of the aura and eventually manifest as physical disease. This process usually takes about three years – it is often seen that some-one presenting with disease went through emotional trauma, such as losing a loved one, three years earlier.

The third, again structured, layer is the mental body, and energizes our thinking processes. It usually appears yellow and extends up to 8in (20cm) from the physical body. As with the emotional layer, mental issues such as confused thinking, excessive fears or worry and chronic trouble in under-standing, if not detected in this layer of the aura, can penetrate the lower layers and after some time develop as a mental health issue in the physical body.

The fourth layer of the aura is the astral level and it fuels our ability to love and relate to others. This layer is the most important layer in healing, as it is the bridge between the lower vibrations of the lower layers and the earth energy to the higher layers and spiritual energy. This layer relates to the heart, which explains why opening ourselves to love, and extending unconditional love to all, is so important in our spiritual development.

The four layers described above are the layers that we use in healing. There are at least three more layers, which relate to our spiritual well-being and support the lower layers on the spiritual plane: the etheric template, which sup-ports the first layer; the celestial body, which supports the emotional layer and the causal body, which supports the mental layer.

All the layers of the aura in total extend about 3ft (1m) beyond the phys-ical body. However the aura is not static, and can be extended or retracted both consciously and sub-consciously. For example, when you are in a crowd you will naturally retract your aura so that it touches as few people as possible. But when you are out in nature you tend to let your aura expand to interact with the environment as much as possible.

No matter how healthy a person appears, they will almost certainly have blocks and tears in their aura, or areas of stagnant and unhealthy Ki. In a later chapter you will learn how to feel for any such issues in the aura. You can then use Reiki to heal them before they develop into illness or disease in the physical body.

How to Feel Your Aura

Most people can learn to see auras, but this does take some time. However, learning to feel the aura is much easier. Start by rubbing your hands together briskly to build their sensitivity. After half a minute or so hold your hands with palms facing each other, and hands as flat as possible, about shoulder width apart. Slowly bring your hands together, until you feel a very slight resistance. It is a very faint feeling and it may help your awareness if you try this with your eyes closed. When you find the first layer of the aura it usually feels like you are trying to push two magnets together. The second, unstructured, layer feels much more spongy. When you feel the resistance, open your eyes and see how far apart your hands are. If they are about 2in (5cm) apart you have found the first layer of your aura! If they are further apart you have found one of the other layers. The more you practice this on yourself the more sensitive you will become, so that you will be able to feel inconsistencies in others' auras and gain information that you can use in healing.

THE SEVEN MAJOR CHAKRAS

In order to be in our best health it is important that as much Ki as possible circulates freely around the body, through each of the layers of the aura and between the aura and the environment around us. As our heart keeps blood pumping around our bodies, it is the chakras that keep energy circulating. Chakra is a Sanskrit word that means 'wheel' and they move energy by spinning. The spinning of the chakra creates a whirlwind effect, which circulates the energy through the different layers of the aura and the physical body.

Chakras come in pairs, each opening at both the front and back of the body, and connecting in the middle within our physical bodies. Each chakra is connected to the others through a series of channels known as meridians or *nadis*, which distribute the energy around the body. We have many chakras, but some are more significant than others. In Reiki we are concerned with the seven main chakras situated along the spine and in the head, and four additional chakras in the palms of our hands and the soles of our feet.

Each chakra extends through each layer of the aura, and supports different parts of the body on a physical, emotional, mental and spiritual level. When a chakra is not functioning properly, an associated lack of health or vitality will be found. Each chakra vibrates at a different level, and therefore associates with a different colour and sound. (You will find a table of correspondences for each of the chakras at Appendix A.)

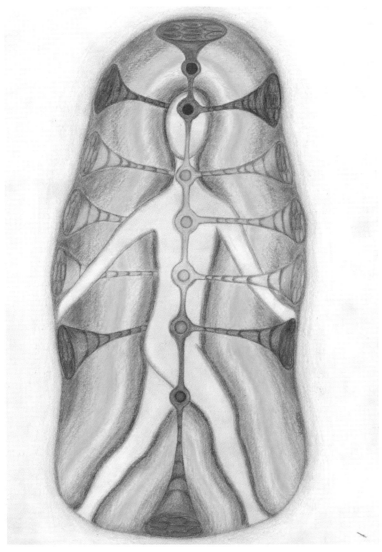

Artist's impression of the aura and chakra system.

The root chakra is the first chakra. It is the lowest vibration, associates with the colour red, the sound Laa and the musical note C. It is located at the perineum and it faces downwards, linking us to the Earth's energy. As it has no front and back it is often considered to be paired with chakra 7, the crown chakra.

Physical – skeletal, kidney, large intestine, legs, feet

Glandular – adrenal

Mental/emotional – vitality, grounding, survival

Malfunction – constipation, haemorrhoids, arthritis, joint pain

The sacral chakra is the second chakra, which associates with the colour orange, the note D and the sound Ba. It is about two or three finger widths below the belly button.

Physical – reproductive system, kidney, bladder

Glandular – gonads

Mental/emotional – desire, libido, pleasure

Malfunction – impotence, frigidity, lower back pain

The solar plexus chakra is the third chakra, is yellow, and is just at the diaphragm under the ribcage. It responds to the note E and the sound Ra.

Physical – stomach, liver, gall bladder, nervous system, muscles

Glandular – pancreas

Mental/emotional – willpower, confidence

Malfunction – anxiety, fatigue, mouth ulcers, diabetes

The heart chakra is located at the heart, is green, has the note F and the sound Yam.

Physical – heart, lungs, blood, circulatory system, arms, hands

Glandular – thymus

Mental/emotional – universal love, empathy, compassion

Malfunction – high blood pressure, heart disease, lung disease

The throat chakra is the fourth chakra, which is light blue and the centre of communication.

Physical – neck, teeth, jaw, shoulders, alimentary canal

Glandular – thyroid, parathyroid

Mental/emotional – expression, creativity, communication

Malfunction – sore throat, stiff neck, colds, deafness, thyroid

The third eye chakra is in the middle of the forehead and responds to indigo, the note A and the sound Ah.

Physical – lower brain, left eye, ears, nose, nervous system

Glandular – pineal

Mental/emotional – visualization, psychic ability, intuition

Malfunction – poor vision, headaches, insomnia, amnesia

Finally *the crown chakra,* at the top of the head, faces upwards and links us to spiritual energy. It is the highest vibration, and responds to violet, the note B and the sound Om.

Physical – upper brain, right eye

Glandular – pituitary

Mental/emotional – understanding, boundlessness

Malfunction – depression, boredom, apathy, Alzheimer's, epilepsy

The Function of the Chakras in Healing

A chakra that is working well spins in a perfect circle, either clockwise or anti-clockwise, and for optimum health each chakra should be in balance spinning at the same rate. However, chakras

How to Test Chakras

Using a pendulum.

You can use a pendulum to test how a chakra is operating. A pendulum used in healing is usually a crystal on a lightweight chain, but can be almost anything that has weight on a chain or string.

Most pendulums have a chain that is longer than you need, so allow the spare to coil in the palm of your hand. Hold the pendulum as lightly as you can between your forefinger and thumb, in line with the chain hanging downwards, about 3in (8cm) above the weight. Take care not to loop the chain over your thumb or forefinger.

Then hold the pendulum 2–4in (5–10cm) above the chakra. The pendulum will soon catch in the flow of the energy and will trace a shape. A perfectly working chakra will produce a perfect circle, spinning either clockwise or anti-clockwise. A straight line indicates a closed chakra. An ellipse shows a chakra that is working but off-centre. If your pendulum doesn't move you are not in the correct location – just move your hand a little bit and then when you finally find the chakra, the pendulum will start moving one way or another.

As soon as your pendulum traces a shape take note of both the shape and how much the pendulum is moving. You can then move on to the next chakra. If you leave the pendulum in place too long it will start to influence the chakra, and you will get an inconsistent reading.

When you move the pendulum from one chakra to another make sure it stills in between. You can use your other hand to stop it.

can become blocked, either spinning off-centre or, in extreme cases, closed or blocked and not spinning at all.

A Reiki healing will open closed chakras and bring the chakras into alignment and balance. It is usual to test all the chakras at the beginning of a healing, note any that are not working perfectly and re-test them at the end of the healing. This is a tangible way of showing your client that the Reiki has worked.

5

GROUNDING, CLEANSING AND PROTECTION

GROUNDING

The soles of your feet have more nerve endings per square inch than any other part of your body. When our skin is in direct contact with the earth, these nerve endings allow us to connect to the energy field on the surface of the earth. Through this physical process of grounding, sometimes called earthing, free electrons from the earth's surface enter our bodies where they have an anti-inflammatory and anti-oxidant effect.

When we are properly grounded our minds are clear and we are 'in the moment'. We are completely present in our bodies, solid and able to concentrate and focus easily.

However, many of us spend the majority of our time completely cut off from this electrical contact with the earth, wearing shoes with rubber soles, walking on carpets made of nylon and sleeping on beds lifted off the ground.

The effect of being ungrounded is to feel slightly behind the curve; scatty, punchy, without focus, daydreaming,

maybe even dizzy, lightheaded and slightly nauseous. Being un-grounded can make you feel a bit jet-lagged.

Those of us who are trying to grow energetically or spiritually often mistakenly think that in order to be more intuitive, more psychic perhaps, we need to be less grounded, to be more 'in our heads', away on some astral plane. But it is actually the opposite. The more grounded you can be, the more focused and present you will be and the more awareness you will have of the energy that you are working with. Empaths, people who are very sensitive to energy, can go into psychic overload if they are exposed to too many higher vibrations. Frequent grounding can be a saviour in this situation.

It is possible to buy grounding mats, to sleep on or to put under your desk, which are plugged into the earth of an electric socket to create the earthing connection. However, simply taking off your shoes and socks and walking barefoot on grass or rock is very grounding, especially if the grass or rock is damp. As a compromise, wearing shoes with leather soles will enable you to retain the earthing connection. There are many other methods of grounding; eating and drinking are both grounding, as is spending time in nature and gardening. If you need to rapidly regain your grounding, try stamping your feet or clapping your hands. If you find that you are regularly un-grounded try carrying a dark- or red-coloured crystal with you in your pocket. Haematite, garnet or smoky quartz are all good for grounding.

When you work with Reiki, either in healing or to develop spiritually, you will find that it is easy to become less grounded. In addition, when you give someone Reiki they are very likely to become ungrounded. So it is important

Artist's impression of grounding.

to know how to stay grounded yourself and also how to ground recipients at the end of a healing.

To ground yourself discreetly and quietly no matter where you are, sit or stand with the soles of your feet flat on the floor. Bring your focus to your feet, feel the contact with the floor. Then imagine that, like a tree, you can grow roots from the soles of your feet down into the earth. Imagine those roots extending down, dividing, spreading and continuing to grow, deep down into the earth, connecting you to the earth energy and anchoring you to the ground. It doesn't matter if you are several floors above the ground, or if there are several layers of concrete between you and the ground; the roots can grow down to the earth, and then deep down into the earth. Allow the roots to continue to divide and grow, pushing aside soil and small stones all the way to the centre of the Earth. If your roots find a large rock you might even wrap a root around it. Take a deep breath and relax. You are now perfectly grounded.

When you are giving Reiki, whether to yourself or to someone else, you will need to ground yourself before and after every healing. You might even need to re-ground yourself during a healing. If you find yourself feeling detached, or any of the other symptoms described above, simply take a moment to focus on re-growing your roots and then carry on with the healing.

At the end of every healing you need to make sure that the recipient is grounded. If they are lying down, you can apply gentle pressure to the soles of their feet, just below the knuckle of the big toe (*see* the photograph on page 57). If they are sat in a chair, you can place your hands on the tops of their feet and apply gentle downward pressure (*see* the photograph on page 62). In either position, when you are applying pressure imagine the

---

Test your Grounding with a Friend

This is a fun way to show how effective simply visualizing your grounding can be.

Stand with your feet firmly planted on the floor, and ground yourself using the root-growing technique described above. When you feel very grounded, ask your friend to give you a gentle shove sideways on your shoulder. When they realize how solidly you are connected to the ground they may give you a couple of extra shoves slightly less gently!!

Then imagine a knife cutting your roots where they meet the ground, completely removing your energetic connection. Then ask your friend to gently push you again. Really gently this time as you will certainly lose your balance!

Always end by re-grounding yourself. Swap places to see how it feels.

recipient growing roots down into the ground. Grounding of itself is very healing, so feel free to spend several minutes in this position, but try to spend at least half a minute. If you have given a long healing, make sure the recipient drinks plenty of water to complete the grounding process.

Cleansing and Protection

Although the outermost layer of our aura has an energetic barrier of sorts, Ki constantly flows in and out of our aura, exchanging energy with our environment and the people around us. Lovers will exchange blobs of Ki, especially from around the heart and sacral chakras; parents of young children will attach cords from their chakras to their child's corresponding chakras over which Ki is exchanged, even when they are not physically close together. These exchanges of Ki are healthy and beneficial to all concerned.

The more you work with Reiki the healthier and more vibrant your aura will become. Some individuals, either consciously or unconsciously, will seek either to take some of your energy for themselves, or to offload some of their less healthy Ki onto you. Although you may not have understood what was happening energetically before, there will be people whom you know that leave you exhausted and drained after spending only ten minutes in their company. We call these people 'energy vampires'! Additionally, if you are particularly empathic, you may often find yourself taking on other people's troubles and issues (and subconsciously therefore, some of their Ki).

As energy workers, it is our responsibility to keep an appropriate distance energetically between ourselves and others. The distance you keep will depend upon your relationship, but unless the relationship is a close personal one you should not take on other's Ki, let others take your Ki except where you are prepared to give it in healing, nor transport one person's Ki to another.

For these reasons, it is our responsibility to keep our auras clean and clear of negative Ki. So we need to regularly cleanse our auras, and keep a layer of protection in place. This will enable us to function better as healers, and will ensure that we don't allow unhealthy Ki to move from one recipient to another.

Cleansing

Reiki is always clean and pure and working to our highest good. But sometimes your body can pick up heavier energies from people or negative situations that can weigh you down. With this in mind, similar to the way that you take a shower when you wake up in the morning, you need to be able to cleanse your aura of Ki that you pick up that isn't yours or doesn't serve your highest good.

The easiest way to clear your aura is simply to sweep it. Using both hands, sweep all over your body as if you are sweeping away dust or breadcrumbs. Start over your head and work down the front and sides of your body, as far around your back as you can reach, and down to your hips and legs. This sweeping can be done just against the skin (it works through clothing) or in the first layer of the aura. Periodically as you sweep, simply flick your hands to the floor so that all of the stagnant energy you have swept out of your aura will fall onto the floor and be neutralized by the earth. You may want to repeat the process through other layers of your aura. Once you have finished, rub your hands together as if you were washing them and do one final flick to the floor. This is an energetic shower that will cleanse your aura and boost your personal energy.

It is important to sweep your aura before and after you give anyone a treatment. Be especially careful to clear your aura in-between treatments. Sweeping the aura not only strengthens your healing energy, but also effectively detaches you from the person you were healing or the activity you were doing before, ensuring that you don't bring someone else's energy onto the next person you are healing.

Kenyoko-Ho – Dry Bathing

Kenyoko-Ho is the Japanese method for clearing the aura. Starting with your right hand on your left shoulder, while exhaling, sweep your hand down and across your body to the opposite hip. End with a little flick to send any negative energy down to the ground to be neutralized. Then place your left hand on your right shoulder and, again whilst exhaling, sweep down and across your body this time to your left hip and end with the flick. Then for the third time, repeat the sweep from left shoulder to right hip and flick with an out-breath.

The second part of the method is to sweep the aura around your arms. When you are healing, your arms will inevitably be in the recipient's aura and can easily pick up their Ki. Form your right hand into a backwards 'C' shape, and starting with your right thumb tucked into the left armpit, while exhaling sweep your right hand down the left arm all the way to the fingertips, the thumb of the right hand travelling down the yin, inside of the arm and fingers, and the fingers of the right hand sweeping down the yang, outside of the arm. As before give a little flick at the end of the movement. Repeat the sweep movement with the left hand sweeping the right arm and flick, and repeat again, for the third sweep, the sweep of the left arm by the right hand and flick, again with an out-breath for each sweep.

This method can be performed slowly and meditatively, one sweep for each out-breath (the whole method therefore taking six breaths to complete). Alternatively, you may decide to do it in two separate breaths, doing the three sweeps of your torso in one out-breath and the three sweeps of your arms in the second out-breath. Or you can perform the whole method very rapidly, all six sweeps in one out-breath.

On the face of it, this method may seem too simple to be very effective. However, it is because of its simplicity and effectiveness that it is used often in other healing methods, such as Qi-gong. When you sweep across your torso you start at the shoulder, where we carry a lot of tension, and then quickly move across the collarbone where a number of acupuncture meridians begin. We then cross breast tissue, lung, heart, stomach, and liver. Finally we end at the hip, where we get a lot of stiffness and even osteoporosis. All of these areas receive an energetic massage.

You might wonder why the method is performed in sets of three, rather than equally on each side. This is a Japanese technique, and in Japan the number four is an unlucky number, because the word for the number four is the same as the word for death. Instead, three is the number of divine perfection.

Protection

Reiki is completely safe, and can do no harm. But we need to take steps to protect our aura; to prevent others taking energy we don't want to share, or putting their negative energy onto us.

The simplest way to create protection is to imagine yourself completely enclosed within a huge soap bubble. By definition a soap bubble is clean, and when it catches the light it incorporates all of the colours of the chakras. Set the intention that negative energy, negative thoughts and negative intentions directed at you, and anything that does not serve you simply bounces off the bubble (this bubble doesn't pop!) and falls to the earth where it is neutralized. Equally, set the intention that the only energy that can go out through the bubble is the energy that you are prepared to share.

It is easy to add enhancements to the bubble visualization. You can add layers of various colours, varying materials, such as Teflon or chicken wire, you could even add a mirror layer to reflect back any negativity that is aimed at you. Once you are happy with your bubble, imagine yourself safe and sound within it.

If you prefer, you can imagine that you have a cloak of protection that performs the same function. If you find visualization difficult you might find this method more effective, and you can literally use your arms to haul the cloak over and around you. Make sure that you are completely enveloped by your cloak, that it goes over your head, around both back and front and under your feet.

You should get into the habit of putting on your protection first thing every morning, with the intention that it will keep you protected all day. But you should also renew the protection whenever you remember through the day. Make a particular point to renew your protection, and add any layers that you feel appropriate, if you are in an environment with a lot of negative energy such as a hospital or shopping centre.

It is essential that you put your protection in place before every healing.

Once you have Reiki II, you can use the Power symbol for protection.

For personal protection draw a life-size symbol in the air in front of you and either step into it, or waft it back over yourself. You can draw the symbol over other people and animals to protect them; you can draw it over your house, car and any other possessions to protect them.

6

HEALING OTHERS

FULL REIKI TREATMENT

AReiki healing can take many different formats, from a full hour-long treatment given in a healing centre or spa, through to a ten- to fifteen-minute healing given to your child whilst reading them a story at bedtime, to first aid given on the side of the road after an accident. Here I will describe the steps you need to take to give a full, planned, hour-long healing in a treatment room. But don't lose sight of the fact that one of the most wonderful things about Reiki is that it can be given at any time, anywhere, and you don't *need* any equipment.

The preparation steps detailed below for the room and for yourself can be done before the patient is present.

Prepare the Room

If you are fortunate enough to have a dedicated room for giving healings you can enjoy setting it up with beautiful fabrics, cushions, blankets, plants and crystals. But all you really need is a space that is clean and tidy.

Before giving Reiki you must make sure that the room is energetically clear. You can do this by smudging, burning incense, playing healing music or a singing bowl or any combination of these. If you have Reiki II you will draw the Power symbol over each wall, the floor, the ceiling and the chair or table you are going to use for healing, and the Harmony symbol into each corner.

Smudging

Smudging is the burning of cleansing herbs to dispel negative energy, and it can be done to cleanse a room, an item (such as a crystal perhaps) or even a person's aura. All you really need are sprigs of dried cleansing herbs such as white sage (healing), juniper (protective), rosemary (soothing) or lavender (relaxing) and a match, candle or lighter. Use the flame to light the herb, then after a few seconds blow out the flame, leaving the herb smoking. It is the smoke that is used for cleansing.

Smudging set. From the top, moving clockwise: smudging stick, white sage, palo santo, all sitting in an abalone shell.

You can buy or make smudging sticks. They are bundles of herbs, either one type or a combination, bound tightly together with cotton thread while still fresh, and then left to dry. If you are making your own, try adding lavender flower heads or rose petals to decorate the sticks. You can also buy smudging sets, which allow you to incorporate the elements into your cleansing ritual. As well as the sticks, the set might include an abalone shell (to represent the water element) to burn the herbs in, and a feather (to represent air) to waft the smoke. When used with the herb (which represents earth) all elements are represented once the herb is set on fire.

To smudge, waft the smoke around the room. If you have Reiki II you can trace the shape of the symbols with the smudge stick and recite the mantra. If you don't have Reiki II, chant an appropriate phrase such as 'I cleanse this space of all negative influence, leaving a positive atmosphere, refreshed and renewed'. When you are using a smudging set, burn the herbs in the abalone shell and use the feather to waft the smoke around the room.

If you are using sage, I advise that you cleanse the room some time before your patient arrives as the smoke is quite heavy and can irritate some people's breathing.

You also need to decide whether your recipient is going to be lying down or sitting in a chair. If a chair, then any kind of chair can be used, although a smaller chair will make it easier for you. If you do not have a treatment table, but you want the recipient to be lying down, a normal bed does not work well as it is too low for you to bend down to, and if you kneel on the floor it is difficult for you to reach the other side of your patient. Much better is to just place a few folded blankets onto a sturdy kitchen or dining room table. You can, of course, simply put blankets or a mattress on the floor provided it is comfortable enough for you.

Prepare Yourself

Before your patient arrives, prepare yourself for giving a treatment. Make sure you are clean and tidy, not wearing any scent, and not wearing jewellery other than your engagement/wedding rings. Wash your hands.

Take time to make sure you are centred; if you have time you could give yourself a Reiki treatment, or spend some time in meditation. At the very least quieten your mind and take three deep breaths, make sure you are grounded, that your aura is clear and that you have your protection in place (*see* Chapter 5, Grounding, Cleansing and Protection). Invite in any deities that you pray to, your angels or spirit guides and those of your patient, and your Reiki guides.

Once your patient has arrived, you can silence your phone.

Prepare Your Patient

Your patient also needs to remove any jewellery other than engagement/wedding rings. Reiki will penetrate through clothing and blankets, so let them know that, other than belts (because of the metal buckle) and probably shoes, there is no need to remove any clothing.

You will need to give a brief description of what Reiki is and help them understand what they can expect from the healing.

Reiki can either be given by placing your hands on the body, or by working 'hands-off' in the aura or a combination of both. It is worth discussing this in advance so that your patient isn't waiting for your touch if you are working hands-off, or so that you have permission to work 'hands-on'.

The Treatment

Once your recipient is settled on the chair or table that you are using for healing make sure that you are grounded, that your aura is clear and that you have your protection in place. You should then set an intention for the healing. The intention will usually be something general, but can be used to request particular healing. If you are intending to give a specific rather than general healing you can set an intention for that, but be careful not to focus on the disease, only the healing of it. If you are offering Reiki for personal

---

Hands-on v Hands-off

In every class I teach I ask students that have received a Reiki healing whether it was 'hands-on' (touching the skin), or 'hands-off' (working in the aura). The answer is usually a 50:50 split.

Realistically, if you are healing on a table and you want to use the 'back of the head' hand position then you will have no choice but to touch there, and it is also usual to touch the feet for grounding. Other than that, it is usually a matter of choice for healer and recipient.

If you work in the aura you may be able to pick up information on the state of the aura by feeling it. So, for example, you may feel areas that are hot or cold, or areas where the aura is uneven or even torn. If you are working hands-on then you will just feel the physical body; so more information can usually be gleaned by the healer working hands-off.

However, there are times where the simple act of a loving touch, for example with a recipient who is lonely or feels unloved, can itself be powerfully healing. In this instance I would choose to work hands-on.

Examples of Intentions for Healing

- General healing:

  'It is my intention to give [name] a full Reiki healing to their highest good'

  'I intend for my ego to step aside and to let Reiki flow for the highest and greatest good'

  'Love, Healing, Compassion'

'I heal with love'

'I ask Reiki to bring health and well-being to balance and harmonize mind, body and spirit'

- Specific healing:

  '[Name's] head is clear and pain-free'

  'It is my intention that [name's] joints move freely and easily'

---

development or in a coaching scenario you could use an affirmation that you have agreed with your client beforehand.

Although it is not essential to the healing, if the patient is lying down this is a nice opportunity to check the operation of their chakras using a dowsing pendulum (*see* Chapter 4, How to Test Chakras). Re-checking the chakras at the end of the healing and finding them more open is a nice convincer for the recipient.

Hand Positions When Patient is Lying Face Up

This is the most common way of giving a full Reiki healing, with the patient lying face up on a table or the floor, and using a series of hand positions.

I teach a series of twelve set hand positions, which will ensure that (a) you cover all areas of the physical body that might be in need of healing, (b) you clear any energy blocks that might be present, and (c) your patient is fully grounded at the end of the healing. Working through the set hand positions also gives your conscious mind something to think

about to help prevent your mind from wandering, and to allow your sub-conscious to come through more easily. I highly recommend that you start by using these positions until you become more experienced at giving Reiki. As you become more experienced with Reiki you will probably find you know intuitively where healing is needed, and you should feel free to follow that guidance. The only areas where it is never acceptable to work is hands-on on the throat, breasts or genitals.

The main objective of the full healing on a table is to cover as much of the physical body as possible. If you are using the set hand positions, it doesn't particularly matter the order in which you do them, although to flow from one to the other moving down the body is the most relaxing for the recipient and seems the most natural. If your recipient is awake and curious, then starting at the head will allow them to see what you are doing without straining. Also, the back of the head hand position is the most intrusive (the recipient usually needs to lift their head so you can put your hands in place), so it is often best done before they are completely relaxed.

This is a description of the hand positions in the order that I usually do them. If I have a patient that doesn't naturally close their eyes I do move to the eyes as the second position, as your hands over their eyes will usually encourage them to close their eyes and relax!

Four Positions on the Head

For these positions you need to position yourself at the top of the treatment table. You can sit or stand, whichever is most comfortable for you.

1. *Back of the head* – I usually use this position first; it is quite invasive for

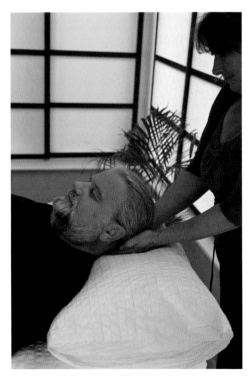

Back of the head.

the patient as they will need to lift their head to allow you to slip your hands underneath. If your patient is already asleep, then push down into the pillow and slide your hands underneath just as far as possible.

2. *Ears and temples* – this is a position where the Reiki often flows very strongly, so if working hands-on rest the fingertips and heel of the hand very gently, keeping the palm away, and if working hands-off keep your hands about 3–4in (8–10cm) from the head.

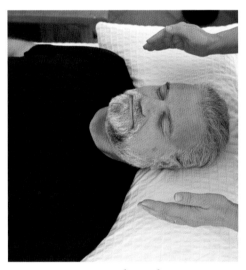

Ears and temples.

3. *Eyes* – here you want to cover both eyes and the third eye chakra. Put your hands together so that the full length of the index fingers are touching, and cross over and fold in your thumbs at the back. Keep your hands high enough off the face that you are in no danger of touching the patient's nose. It is unusual to work hands-on

in this position, but if you really wanted to you could lightly rest the heels of your hands on the hairline and fingertips on the cheek-bones.

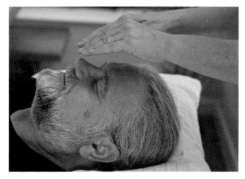

Eyes.

4. *Under the chin* – this position should always be hands-off as having your throat touched feels threatening. Reach your hands forward to meet under the chin, taking great care not to touch the throat. Overlap your fingertips sufficiently so there is no gap between the shorter fingers of each hand. It is acceptable to rest your elbows on the pillow to make this position more comfortable for you.

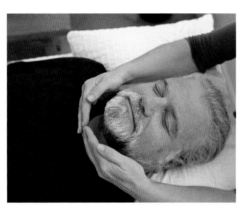

Under the chin.

Four Positions on the Torso

For these positions you will need to stand to the side of the treatment table. Swapping the hand that is working on the far side of the patient now and again will ease your lower back.

1. *Upper chest* – to cover as much of the upper chest as possible without touching the throat, you need to make a 'V' with your hands. Hold your near-side hand at an angle with the heel of your hand at the top of the shoulder and the fingers pointing to the sternum, then place the heel of your far-side hand at the tip of the fingers of your other hand, with your fingers at the top of the patient's other shoulder.

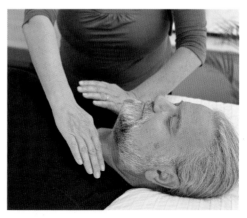

Upper chest.

2. *Chest* – place your hands one in front of the other in a straight line over the rib cage.

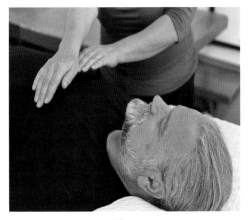

Chest.

3. *Stomach* – keeping your hands in a straight line, move down along the torso to cover the stomach area.

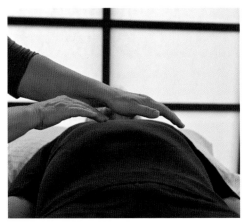

Stomach.

4. *Abdomen* – to cover the abdomen as much as possible without touching the genitals make the opposite 'V' with your hands. Hold your near-side hand at an angle with the heel of your hand at the hip crease and the fingers pointing to the navel, then place the heel of your far-side hand at the tip of the fingers of your other hand over the navel, with your fingers pointing to the far hip crease. Working hands-off in this area may be more comfortable for both you and your patient. The alternative if working hands-on is to simply place a hand on each hip and give healing in that position.

Abdomen.

Four Positions on the Legs

Not all teachers teach hand positions on the legs, but energy blocks often form in the thighs and knees, so I include the legs in all my healings. You will need to start standing to the side for the knees, then move to the foot of the table for the ankles and feet. At the end of the table it should be possible for you to sit again.

1. *Knees* – simply use one hand for each knee.

Knees.

2. *Ankles* – you can stay at the side of the table and use one hand for each ankle as with the knees. I prefer to sit at the foot end, to rest my forearms against the end of the table and to cup one hand over each ankle.

Ankles.

3. *Tops of the feet* – hold your left hand over the patient's right foot, and your right hand over their left foot.

Left foot.

4. *Soles of the feet* – hold your left hand under patient's right foot, and your right hand under their left foot.

Right foot.

Grounding.

As an alternative to 3 and 4 above, you can put your hand over the top and sole of the patient's feet, one foot at a time.

However you chose to do the feet, and whether working hands-on or hands-off, at the end of the healing apply the thumb of each hand to the area below the knuckle of the big toe on the soles of the feet with the rest of your hand over the top of each foot and apply a gentle pressure. Hold this position for at least half a minute. Use your intention to grow tree roots from your patient's feet down into the ground to ensure that they are grounded.

Hand Positions When Patient is Lying Face Down

There are two schools of thought amongst Reiki Masters concerning whether or not a Reiki treatment should include hand positions on the back. One being that a full treatment should include at least four hand positions on the back along the spine, and the other being that, as Reiki goes where it is needed, and can definitely reach the back of the body from the front of the body, then it is a shame to disturb the patient to ask them to turn over.

The deciding factor for you could be whether the patient suffers with a bad back. It is unusual for a paying client to come for Reiki specifically for a bad back as they are more likely to look to an osteopath or chiropractor. But if you have a friend or family member who suffers with a bad back it is nice to be able to offer them Reiki, in which case you could either do a whole treatment on their back to save disturbing them to turn over, or have them turn over or at least turn onto their side just to add the hand positions on the back. So I also teach optional hand positions with the patient lying on their front for healing the back.

Three Positions on the Head

If you have a table with a cut-out for the face or additional head support that enables the patient to lie face down, then you can use the same hand positions as for a patient lying face up. The back of the head is easy to reach and no longer needs to be hands-on; ears and temples are the same as for face up, for the eyes you will need to put your hands under the table and under the chin becomes base of the head.

As many of you won't have such a table, these are the hand positions for a patient lying with their head turned to one side. You start at the head end of the table, and you can sit on a chair or stool if that is more comfortable for you.

1. *Back of the head and eyes* – place your hands on the table, one in front of the eyes and the other at the back of the head. Even if working generally hands-on, I suggest that the hand on the eyes here be hands-off.

2. *Ears and temples* – you can either work on one side of the head and hold the intention that Reiki flows through to the other side, or put one hand under the table to heal the side of the face that is turned down.

3. *Under the chin* – the hand on the face side does under the chin as normal; the other hand heals the base of the back of the head.

Patient on their side – shoulder blades.

Four Positions on the Back

These positions can be used as part of a full back healing, or can be incorporated into a healing with the patient lying on their back by asking them to turn over onto their back, or at least onto their side and turning back again once these four positions have been done. You will need to stand to the side of the table.

Swapping over which hand is on the far side of the back now and again will ease your lower back.

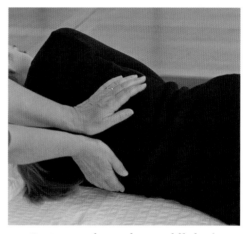

Patient on their side – middle back.

1. *Shoulder blades* – place your hands one in front of the other in a straight line across the top of the back.

2. *Middle back* – place one hand in front of the other about a third of the way down the back.

3. *Lower back* – place one hand in front of the other over the lower back.

4. *Coccyx* – place one hand in front of the other at the base of the spine.

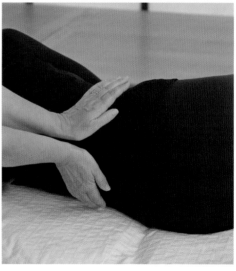

Patient on their side – lower back.

Patient on their side – coccyx.

Patient on their front – lower back.

Patient on their front – coccyx.

Patient on their front – shoulder blades.

Three Positions on the Legs

1. *Back of the knees* – one hand over each knee.

2. *Ankles* – you can stay at the side and use one hand for each ankle as with the knees. I prefer to sit at the foot end, to rest my forearms against the end of the table and to cup one hand over each ankle.

3. *Soles of the feet* – place one hand over the sole of each foot.

At the end of the healing, place the thumb of each hand on the area below the knuckle of the big toe on the soles of the feet and wrap the rest of your hand over the top of each foot and apply a gentle pressure. Hold this position for at

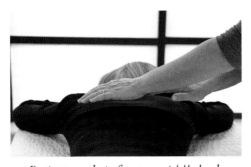

Patient on their front – middle back.

least half a minute. Use your intention to grow tree roots from your patient's feet down into the ground to ensure that they are grounded.

Hand Positions When the Patient is Sat in a Chair

There are several reasons why you might choose to give a treatment in a chair: if you don't have a table and would be physically uncomfortable working on the floor; if you need to give a treatment wherever you happen to be and there is something to sit on; or if your recipient cannot easily get on and off a table. A chair treatment is a perfectly good treatment, especially if you have a comfortable high chair so that the recipient can rest their head.

As every chair is different, and both healers and patients come in many different shapes and sizes, you will need to be quite flexible in how you go about giving a chair healing. The main priority is what is comfortable for you and for your patient. Make sure that you have a cushion to sit or kneel on, and adjust your position as necessary. As it is less easy to reach some areas of the body when the patient is sitting I tend to work through each of the chakras in turn rather than try to cover the whole physical body.

Start standing to the side of your patient. You are going to hold your arms out so that one hand is at your patient's front and the other at the back. One of the advantages of a chair healing is that you can heal the front and back at the same time! I recommend working hands-off in a chair, at least for the chakra positions. With the patient's permission you can work hands-on on the legs, and you will find it more comfortable if you do.

Note that you can put your hand between the patient and the back of the chair if there is room, but that Reiki will go through the chair if there is not. If you get to a point where the patient and chair together are so wide that it is difficult to hold your arms so far apart, then move around to the front and hold both hands in front of the patient's chakra. As you move from the higher to the lower chakras, move from standing to kneeling and/or sitting as is comfortable for you.

Third eye.

Throat.

Heart.

Solar plexus.

Sacral.

Root.

Knees.

Tops of the feet.

1. *Third eye* – hold one hand in front of the patient's third eye in the middle of their forehead and the other at the back of the head.

2. *Throat* – move the hands down so that they are opposite the throat, one at the front and the other at the back.

3. *Heart* – move the hands down so that they are opposite the heart, one at the front, and the other at the back. If you have to bend over, consider moving to kneel on a cushion at this point.

4. *Solar plexus* – move the hands down so that they are opposite the solar plexus at the diaphragm at the bottom of the rib cage, one at the front, and the other at the back.

5. *Sacral* – move the hands down so that they are opposite the sacral chakra about three finger widths below the navel, one at the front, and the other at the back. By now you might find the depth of the chair means that your arms are uncomfortably far apart. Rather than risk touching your patient by accident you can move around to the front and place both hands in front of the sacral chakra.

6. *Root* – move the hands down so that both are in front of the root chakra.

7. *Knees* – it will be much more comfortable here for you to work hands-on, so as long as you have the patient's permission place a hand on each knee.

8. *Tops of the feet* – place a hand on top of each of the feet. Apply gentle downward pressure and in your mind grow roots from the soles of your patient's feet down into the ground for grounding.

'Reiki On'

While giving Reiki, if you are working hands-off in the aura, cup your hands slightly and keep the fingers together so that there are no gaps. If you are working hands-on simply lay your hands flat on the patient. Once you have your hands in position you just think 'Reiki on' and Reiki will start to flow. For Reiki II, to switch Reiki on draw the Power symbol onto the palm of either or both hands before placing them in the aura or on the client. You can re-draw the Power symbol whenever you feel it is needed by gently removing your hand from the client, drawing the symbol and gently placing the hand back.

A full Reiki healing is usually an hour long. The first visit might be longer to allow time for you to take some details from your patient and to discuss any issues they have. You will usually want to spend between three and five minutes on each hand position. If you use the twelve set positions this will give you forty to sixty minutes of healing. Adjust the time per hand position according to the number of hand positions you plan to use and the length of time agreed for the treatment. It is not necessary to spend exactly the same amount of time on each position. If you search on YouTube for 'Reiki Music (three or five) minute bell' you can find recordings that have a bell ring every few minutes to help you keep track of time.

As your sensitivity to Reiki grows, you might start to notice that the Ki ebbs and flows as you give a healing. When you can tune into this, you will notice that the feeling of Reiki in your hands will lessen momentarily, and this is Reiki letting you know it's time to move to the next hand position.

During the Treatment

I am often asked whether you should close your eyes when giving Reiki. I find that I almost always enter a semi-meditative state when I am giving Reiki, and that my eyes go into soft focus. By keeping your eyes open, even if not quite focused, you will be able to see any physical reaction that your patient might have to the healing, such as twitching, which would indicate an energy block. Also with your eyes closed it is hard to keep your balance, and especially if you are standing over the recipient on a table you run the risk of your hands wavering slightly and accidentally touching the recipient.

What you are thinking whilst you are giving Reiki is quite important. When Sensei Usui travelled to India in search of a hands-on healing method, the Gurus he met were puzzled by his focus on physical healing, insisting that healing begins in the mind. We have already seen how this is true for the Reiki recipient, but it is doubly true for the Reiki healer.

Reiki is an intelligent energy, and we can communicate with it through our intention. Although Reiki will always go where it is most needed, we can use our intention to suggest to Reiki where it might go. So most importantly, we must use our intention to direct Reiki to heal. When you are giving Reiki, don't concentrate on the recipient's symptoms, their diagnosis or their disease. Instead intend for them to be healed. Picture them in your mind's eye completely healthy and happy, perhaps being showered with golden light. If you are not a visual person, then repeat an appropriate mantra silently in your mind whilst you are sending Reiki; perhaps 'love, compassion, healing...' or 'I am grateful for the gift of healing – I am grateful for the gift of Reiki...'

You must be especially careful when you are setting an intention for a specific healing that your language focuses on the result and not on the issue. So, for example, instead of 'It is my intention to heal Mary's arthritis' try 'This healing will leave Mary's joints moving freely and with ease'.

Above all, you must have confidence that Reiki can heal. If you believe that Reiki can heal, and you know that you have Reiki, then you know that you can heal! Be grateful for this gift of healing and (although you can never promise a patient a cure), look forward with anticipation to incredible results.

What You Might Feel

Remember that when you are giving Reiki, the healing energy is flowing through you on its way to the recipient. So you are likely to feel calm and relaxed. If you are sensitive to the energy you will feel it moving through your body. You will almost certainly feel Reiki in your hands. The majority of people feel this as heat, but you may feel it as tingling, pins and needles, swirling or spinning, you may even feel it as cold. You may always feel the same sensation in your hands, or

most likely, especially as you develop, the sensations will be different for different recipients, and even for the same recipient on different occasions. As your sensitivity develops you may also start to feel Reiki flowing from your feet, your eyes or from your heart chakra.

As you work with Reiki more you will become more intuitive and you might start to receive information while you are giving Reiki. This could be in the form of colours or pictures if you are a visual person, in the form of sounds if you are more auditory or even in the form of fragrances or tastes. You might just get a sense of knowing.

During the treatment you might suddenly become aware of an ache or pain, or a particular emotion. It might be your pain or emotion (and remember, while you are giving Reiki it is also flowing through you, so you often receive healing yourself), or it may be that you are being shown the symptoms of your patient or what they are feeling from the healing. This can be a little worrying, but it is quite normal. To find out if the pain belongs to you or to the recipient, stop giving Reiki for a moment. If the pain stops, then it is theirs. If it goes on, then it is yours. If it is yours, be sure to give yourself Reiki after the healing. If it is theirs, this experience often occurs when a patient is not aware of, or cannot describe, the symptoms; it is usually a sign that perhaps something other than Reiki could be beneficial to the patient, for example something that should be brought to the attention of their GP. Be thankful that you have been given this sensory experience, and for the

Byosen Scanning

As your ability to feel or even see the aura increases you can begin to use this awareness in healing. Place both hands an inch or two away from the recipient's body and find that feeling of resistance that indicates you have found the edge of a layer of the aura. Move the hands over this layer, noting how closely the layer follows the contours of the body or whether there are areas that bulge away from the body or where there are even gaps or tears in the layer. You may also start to notice areas of heat and coldness. Then take note of texture finding areas that are perhaps prickly, sticky or dense. You can do this in the first three layers of the aura.

Areas of heat usually indicate that healing is needed in this area – the heat being caused by the body's own Ki being present, whereas areas of cold usually indicate an old injury. Sticky or dense areas usually indicate an energy block, or energy that is not beneficial which should be removed. Reiki will clear these areas, but if you are Reiki II or over using psychic surgery can speed up the process.

Gently and sensitively discuss your findings with the patient and build your own glossary of what these phenomena in the different layers of the aura mean for a person's physical, emotional, mental and spiritual health and well-being.

opportunity this gives you to help and understand your patient. Once you are aware of the sensation, kindly say to the Universe (in your mind) 'Thank you for making me aware of these symptoms. Now please take them away with love and light.' You can then continue with the healing. Make a point to discuss these symptoms with the patient after the healing.

As your sensitivity to Ki increases you will start to become increasingly aware of what the aura feels like, and you can use a technique called byosen scanning to read from the aura what healing is needed.

What the Patient Might Feel

What the recipient will feel will depend upon how sensitive they are to Ki. Almost everyone will at least feel very calm and relaxed, and most will feel a sensation of heat from your hands. But some people can have quite distinct sensations including feeling the Ki move through the body, lightness, a feeling of levitation, seeing colours, hearing music, even meeting a passed loved one. It is not unusual for the patient to feel that you were touching them even when you weren't, or that you were working on a different part of the body than you actually were. This is all evidence that the Reiki goes where it is needed. Unless you are very perceptive you will not usually be aware of the experiences that your patient is having and so this is usually something that you will discuss after the healing.

During the healing there are visual indications to look out for. The patient's breathing may become heavier or lighter but it will usually slow as they relax. As the Reiki moves through the tanden, the energy centre in the abdomen where Reiki is stored, there will often be tummy rumbling. Reiki might clear some energy blocks, which can manifest physically as twitching or emotionally as tears or giggling. Take all these as signs that Reiki is doing its work and just continue to give healing.

After the Healing

Grounding

Always close the healing by applying firm pressure to the soles of the recipient's feet for at least half a minute to make sure that they are grounded. Reiki is so incredibly safe that you really can't do anything wrong when giving Reiki, but by far the most dangerous thing you can do is send your patient away before they are properly grounded, especially if they are driving.

Re-Check the Chakras

If you checked the chakras at the start, re-test any that weren't functioning perfectly and note the differences.

Sweep the Aura

If you have done a full face-to-face healing on a table then it is nice to smooth the recipient's aura. Starting at the head and with the flats of your hands and forearms gently sweep through the aura about 2in (5cm) above the body down to the feet. Intend that you are clearing any debris out of the aura, and when you get to the feet give a little flick towards the floor, sending anything negative down to the earth to be neutralized. Do this once down the front of the body and once each side.

Once you have woken your patient, offer a drink of water to further ground them. You should then take some time to discuss the recipient's experiences. As well as giving you valuable information about the healing and your patient's experience, this also gives you the opportunity to assess if they are well grounded.

How Many Treatments?

It is worth at this point considering what exactly is meant by the word 'healing'. The word 'heal' comes from the Old English 'haelan', which itself derives from the Proto-German 'hailjan', literally 'to make whole'.[7] Traditionally with allopathic or Western medicine the objective is usually to attain physical healing. Little if any consideration is given to the mind and spirit. But Reiki is a holistic therapy, and so whenever healing is given, it is on a physical, mental, emotional and spiritual level and this is what is meant by 'healing' in connection to Reiki.

Although I spend a lot of time teaching a set of hand positions for giving Reiki, Reiki is an intelligent energy, and in truth it goes where it is most needed. If you have a patient who is aware that they are in need of physical healing, but is perhaps not aware that they need emotional or spiritual healing, then sometimes they are disappointed that the physical healing is not instant.

Reiki is miraculous. To be able to give healing with little or no actual physical contact, and with no risk of side-effects, is truly miraculous. But to expect an instant cure is not realistic. Because Reiki is healing on every level, almost everyone you heal will need a number of treatments to see an improvement in their condition. It is best to set this expectation in the early days, to ensure that your patient is not disappointed.

When Mrs Takata attended Hayashi's clinic in Tokyo her asthma, gallstones and tumour were all completely healed. But she received Reiki daily for four months. This seems a long time, but in fact it was probably no longer than it would have taken her body to fully recover from surgery and the after-effects of the anaesthetic; we just aren't used to thinking of surgery that way. So with Reiki your patient must be patient!

Thankfully, most recipients will notice some instant improvement generally even after the first healing. They will have been very relaxed during the healing. They will probably sleep very well the first night after receiving Reiki, and generally be calmer and more tranquil. These feelings can last from twenty-four to forty-eight hours as Reiki continues to work with the body. However, unless more Reiki is received the old patterns will gradually return.

So the sooner a second healing can be given the better. With family and friends that you see often, feel free to give two or even three ten- to twenty-minute healings each day or at least on consecutive days. With clients, or where this frequency might be too intrusive or impractical for either or both of you, then aim to do every other day or at the very least every two or three days. Quite a nice pattern for giving healings to a client is Monday, Wednesday and Friday, or Wednesday,

Friday and Monday. Remember that once you have Reiki II then you can combine face-to-face with distance healings, or indeed conduct all healings as distance healings, making frequent healings more manageable.

In the second healing the Reiki is likely to dig a bit deeper into the recipient's issues, and they can feel a little more unsettled than they did after the first healing. With some people, where either a lot of healing is needed, or where the healing is happening rapidly, then the recipient can have a reaction to the healing, sometimes known as a healing crisis. This makes it sound a bit more dramatic than it is likely to be in practice. It is perhaps comparable to the headaches and spots that you can experience in the early days of a detox programme. Nevertheless it is best for the recipient to push through this period and onto the third healing as quickly as possible. After the third healing these issues are likely to have been resolved and the recipient can just look forward to a steady improvement physically, mentally, emotionally and spiritually. For this reason you should always try to arrange the second and third follow-up treatments either at the time you arrange the first treatment or straight away after the first treatment. If you are charging for the healing, an easy way to do this is to offer a special discount for healings booked in courses of three, such as three for the price of two, or thereabouts. After the initial course of three treatments you can settle into a pattern of one or two treatments per week until the patient is healed.

Be very careful neither to diagnose, nor to promise a particular outcome for your patient. As a Reiki practitioner you are not medically trained. You may receive some intuitive feedback about your patient, but you should be very careful about how or whether you share this information. You cannot promise an overall outcome because you don't actually know what is in the best interests of your patient. You can't even promise an outcome on a treatment-by-treatment level, because although you can set an intention for a healing, you don't know whether the priority for your patient is physical, mental, emotional or spiritual. Only Reiki can know this.

If you are ever working with a patient who is very sick you cannot even promise that Reiki will save their life. Reiki has been successful in saving lives of people with cancer and other very serious diseases. But again, you cannot know that prolonging your patient's life is what is right for their highest and greatest good. It is a fact of life that we all have to die. Healing in this situation can be to take away the physical pain, to take away the emotional fear and to allow the spirit to prepare for its transition.

If your recipient is taking any medication make it clear that they should not make any changes to the dose without first consulting their doctor. Discuss any further action the recipient can take and then agree a day and time for the next healing.

HEALING CHILDREN

When you are healing children Reiki works in exactly the same way, but children don't relax in the same way that adults do, and there are a few things you should bear in mind to make the child as comfortable as possible.

As children are smaller, they will likely need less Reiki than an adult with the same condition. It is also more difficult for a child to stay still for any length of time. So consider giving a higher number of shorter treatments. It is not necessary for the child to stay completely still for the treatment. Consider letting the child choose some music that they find relaxing. I have found that playing an audiobook can help the child to relax.

If you are healing your own child, then adding Reiki to the bedtime routine is a lovely thing to do. You could give Reiki whilst reading a bedtime story, or give Reiki whilst the child falls asleep. It doesn't matter if the child is doing something else when you give Reiki. I have given all my kids Reiki whilst they were watching television, either stood behind the sofa with my hands on their shoulders, or sitting next to them with their feet in my lap.

To explain to a child what Reiki is, there is no reason not to use a favourite sci-fi or fantasy film to help them understand. You might compare Reiki to The Force in *Star Wars* (not the Dark Side of course!), or to magic in Harry Potter.

Tomato Experiment

Put two tomatoes on a plate. Label one as 'Reiki' and the other as 'No Reiki'. At a set time every day give Reiki to the 'Reiki' tomato, but not to the other. Over time the 'No Reiki' tomato will turn bad, while the other tomato will stay healthy for much longer.

To show children that Reiki works you can set up a little experiment, perhaps planting up two pots of seeds, and giving Reiki to one but not the other. The seeds you have Reiki'd will grow faster and stronger.

If the child develops a real interest in Reiki consider allowing them to learn Reiki for themselves. I often think how different my life would have been if I had learned Reiki at a much younger age. Children as young as seven can learn Reiki, particularly in a class designed for children, but do be sure that it is the child's desire to learn, not yours!

SHORTENED TREATMENT

You will not always have time to give an hour-long treatment, and that is fine. Any Reiki – literally a minute or so – is better than no Reiki. If you have twenty-five to thirty minutes you could still go through the standard hand positions, just spending two minutes in each position. However, anything shorter than this will probably not be relaxing for the recipient. So in this case you can either choose a reduced number of the set hand positions and just work through those, or you can adopt a different approach, just choosing one or two hand positions and using those.

To save time, you might give these treatments wherever your recipient happens to be rather than setting up a room for healing. You might just use hand positions that are the most comfortable. So for example, if I was giving my kids Reiki while they were watching television, we had a sofa in our TV room that had space to walk behind it, so I would stand behind them and place my hands on their shoulders and turn 'Reiki on'. If you are sitting on a sofa next to someone it might be easiest just to place one hand on their shoulder and the other on their knee. Or perhaps they lie on the sofa with their feet in your lap and you can give Reiki through their feet.

In these situations we are not giving a full healing, and we are trusting Reiki to go where it is needed. You don't need to follow all of the preparation steps detailed at the beginning of the chapter. You should still take just a few seconds to ground yourself, sweep your aura through and put your protection in place. Other than that, all you need to do is put your hands in place and think 'Reiki on'. At the end, you must just make sure your patient is grounded and that your aura is clear.

FIRST AID

You may find yourself in a situation where you have no time to prepare and where healing is needed immediately. Fortunately with Reiki no tools are needed other than your hands and the only essential preparation takes just seconds.

If you can, wash your hands and use hand sanitizer. If this is not possible, work only in the aura and don't touch the patient.

In a first-aid situation there is no need to remove jewellery, or even belts and shoes, but you do still need to get consent. If the patient is unable to give consent in the usual way you can always ask their higher self, or simply offer Reiki by turning 'Reiki on' and holding the intention that they receive Reiki if they would like it.

It is very important that you don't move the patient. Just work in whichever hand position(s) you can reach. Do not touch any area where you might cause pain, choosing instead to work in the aura. Be aware that, whether you work hands-on or hands-off, most people feel Reiki as heat, so if you are healing a burn, rely on Reiki to go where it is needed, and work hands-off at the nearest area that is not burned.

If you have Reiki II, then working at a short distance and using the Distance symbol to connect is ideal. Reiki will help with pain, shock and bleeding. You may have read elsewhere that Reiki should not be given to a broken bone or severed limb until it has been set or re-attached, the concern being that the healing will start too soon making it impossible to re-set or re-attach, but neither of these fears are grounded. There are no circumstances in which Reiki is not beneficial.

DISTANCE HEALING

Many of us have the sense that there is an unseen connection between ourselves and others; most particularly our loved ones. A parent will have a sense of a child being in trouble; often when you pick up the phone with the intention to call someone you will find that they are ringing you at the same time. Now that we know from modern physics that we are connected and that space and time is not on a continuum as most of us ordinarily experience it, but that it is circular, then it becomes easy to believe that we can send healing to other people, things and places anywhere in the Universe and to any time in history or in the future.

It is important that you recognize that distance healing is not second best to a face-to-face healing. In fact many people find distance healings to be more effective than a face-to-face healing. Whether this is caused by the use of the Distance symbol or whether this is because the recipient can be more relaxed in their own environment I have not yet concluded. But that Sensei Usui chose to heal his clients in a room next door to the room that he was in is confirmation enough.

Distance healing is usually taught at Reiki II, as the Distance symbol makes it incredibly easy for all to send distance healing. However, it is possible to send distance healing if you only have Reiki I. The easiest way to do this is to hold an image, a photograph or picture of who/what you want to send healing to in your cupped hands with one hand below the image and one above, simply think 'Reiki on' and you will be able to send healing. Once you have finished sending Reiki you need to break the connection by rubbing your hands together. If you have Reiki II, you can add the Distance symbol to the image healing method I outlined above. Hold the image in one hand, draw the Distance symbol over the image with your other hand, reciting the mantra three times and hold the intention to make the connection. Then send Reiki as usual.

Full Reiki Treatment (Reiki II)

An additional thing to think about with distance healing is to decide what arrangements you will make to contact your patient. You need to make sure they are ready to receive Reiki, discuss their needs, wake them at the end of the healing, and discuss how the healing went. The choices are to be on a video call with the patient while you send Reiki, to just be on the phone, or to contact the patient before and after but not to have an open line of communication while you are sending. All methods are acceptable, it just depends what works best for you.

Video call. I started using Zoom during the Covid lockdown to send distance healings. You can arrange a time beforehand and set up a video call, and then carry out the healing with the video on. If you think that seeing or being seen on the screen whilst doing the healing might be a bit odd then you or the patient can turn the camera off during the healing, but the patient will still be able to hear you when you wake them at the end.

Telephone. You could phone the patient when you are ready to start, and carry out the healing with the phone line open on speaker so that the patient will hear you when you want to wake them up. If you don't want to keep the phone on, the issue is that your patient will want to turn their phone to silent so that they don't get disturbed by incoming calls during the healing, and then how do you call them to wake them up? The way I have got around this in the past is to have the patient set an alarm to wake themselves up, and then call them after they turn their phone back on. But this does take away some flexibility over the time the treatment will take. However, this method is particularly suitable if your patient wants a treatment before they go to sleep, and you could just arrange to call them to discuss the treatment in the morning.

Remote. There is no need to be in active contact when you send Reiki, so you can simply agree a time and send it at that time with the follow-up to be done later. I have used this method with family members, or very regular clients, but otherwise I always have the concern that the patient might not be sitting quietly at the agreed time and might not notice that they are receiving the Reiki.

Prepare the Room

Of course you don't need to prepare the treatment bed or chair, but you should clear the room energetically. You should also ask your patient to create a pleasant space, to light a candle or incense stick and perhaps to play some soothing music.

Prepare Yourself

This is just the same as for a face-to-face healing.

Prepare Your Patient

This is just the same as for a face-to-face healing, except of course you will only be working hands-off. If you are Reiki II and doing a paid-for healing you will need to work out how to take the client history and get their consent. You might choose to do it on the call or video call, or you might choose to have a separate call beforehand to go over the form. Or you could email or post it to your client and ask them to sign it and send it back. Check whether your insurance company requires an original signature on the consent form, or whether an emailed form or even a note made by you on their record is adequate.

Ask your patient to have a glass of water ready for them to drink at the end of the healing.

The Treatment

Make sure that you are grounded, clear your aura and put your protection in place. Set an intention for the healing, then use one of the following methods for sending distance healing.

Proxy

A very common method in distance healing is the use of a proxy. This method is useful either if you intend to send a full-length healing, as it keeps our conscious mind occupied, or where you want to direct healing to a specific area rather than to a person, thing or place generally.

The proxy is a representative, or stand-in, for the recipient. For healings on people or animals it is common to use a doll or teddy that has a similar shape to the recipient. For example, if you wanted to send healing to someone's broken leg you might use a doll or teddy bear as the proxy and place your hands on the appropriate leg to direct healing there. However, you can also use a cushion or

Using a proxy.

pillow, or even your own body. Start by drawing the Distance symbol and hold the intention that the recipient is represented by the proxy, and will receive the healing that you give via the proxy. It is possible to test the chakras using your pendulum over the proxy in the location of the chakras. You can then go through a full healing using any or all of the standard hand positions, or whichever hand position(s) you are guided to use, and at Reiki II to add symbols as you feel is appropriate.

Visualizing the Patient

If you are good at visualizing, then instead of using an image or a proxy you might prefer to visualize that the recipient is with you receiving Reiki. To make this easier, you can imagine your recipient lying on your treatment couch if you have one, or sitting in a chair. Draw the Distance symbol to make the connection then carry out the table or chair healing in the normal way, moving around the chair or table and placing your hands around your visualized recipient.

Using this method is particularly effective if there are more than one of you sending healing. I once had a lovely experience when four Reiki healers stood around my treatment table sending healing to someone who was in hospital undergoing a lung transplant.

Beaming

You can beam Reiki to a recipient that is in line of sight but more than around 6ft (2m) away from you, or to an image that is propped up in front of you such as a

Beaming.

photo in a photo frame, or via a laptop or computer screen to someone you are on a video call with.

First use the Distance symbol to make the connection, then holding both hands in front of you, palms facing forwards, imagine Reiki beaming from your hands to your intended recipient. When I am doing this I like to think of the Distance symbol acting as a bridge taking the Reiki to where you intend it to go. Again you can send any symbol that you consider appropriate, and I like to imagine the symbol crossing the 'bridge'.

After the Treatment

To send grounding at the end of the healing, apply pressure to the feet of any proxy or to your visualized patient. If you are beaming, just use your intention. You can re-check the chakras, and if you have been using a proxy or a visualized patient you can sweep the aura.

How Many Treatments?

You will find that a distance healing takes less time than a face-to-face healing. Again, whether this is amplification by the Distance symbol or that the recipient is more relaxed I am not certain. But a full distance Reiki healing is often accomplished in about thirty-five to forty minutes. For a recipient who is suffering from a minor ailment, a useful healing can easily be achieved in ten to fifteen minutes.

Little and often is again preferable to sporadic lengthy treatments, and you have the added advantage of your recipient not needing to travel to you. So if it is possible for you and not too disruptive, I would recommend daily fifteen-minute healings. More realistically, especially for a paying client, perhaps forty minutes every other day for at least three healings is the best option.

7

HEALING YOURSELF

Although in the West, Reiki is seen primarily as a method of physical healing, in Japan it is seen as a route to enlightenment, part of a process of spiritual self-development. Even if your primary reason for learning Reiki is to give healing to others, it is very important that you give yourself Reiki often, and that you use Reiki for your own personal development. This is not selfish – it will make you a better healer.

It is a requirement that after your attunement you give yourself Reiki for the next twenty-one days. This is known as the twenty-one-day clearing period. One of the purposes of daily self-healing during the twenty-one-day clearing period is to get you into the habit of daily self-healing. Hopefully the results will be so positive that you will be addicted for life!

The minimum amount of time that you will ideally spend in dedicated self-healing depends upon the level of Reiki you are at: for Reiki I fifteen minutes per day is adequate, and for Reiki II you need to be building up to thirty minutes per day. This is in addition to the time you spend using Reiki as part of your normal life, giving Reiki to your food and drink, giving yourself Reiki whilst watching television, reading a book or just falling asleep. Remember that you can never give yourself too much Reiki.

The preparation steps needed for self-healing are much less than when healing someone else. I will outline here the steps required for a perfect, full Reiki healing. You can remove many of the steps depending upon where you are and how much time you have.

PREPARE THE ROOM

Make sure that the room is energetically clear by smudging, or burning incense or using the symbols if you are Reiki II or above. When healing yourself, you don't have to be indoors. You can give yourself Reiki anywhere. Perhaps experiment with being outside in nature. You could even give yourself a healing travelling home from work on the bus!

PREPARE YOURSELF

You can keep your jewellery on for self-healing. Use a timer if it will enable you to relax more.

Hand Positions for Self-Healing

As for healing others, there are a number of standard hand positions that can be followed which will ensure that Reiki flows to all areas of the body; working through the hand positions also helps you to hold your attention while you carry out your self-healing. However, once you are confident in giving yourself Reiki, feel free to follow your intuition, to skip some positions, add in other positions or indeed just to adopt one or two positions that work for you.

It is fine to work either hands-on or hands-off or a combination of the two in your self-healing. I find hands-off is less tiring on the arms, but I suggest that you try both ways and decide what works best for you at any given time. You can of course do some positions hands-on and some positions hands-off.

Four Positions on the Head

1. *Back of the head* – you can place the hands side by side or one above the other, whichever is most comfortable for you.

2. *Ears and temples* – hold the hands over the ears, the fingertips as close to the temples as is comfortable.

3. *Eyes* – here you want to cover both eyes and the third eye chakra, so lightly rest the heel of your hands on the bone below the eye socket and fingertips on the hairline.

4. *Throat* – put both wrists together and hold them at the throat with the hands extending around the neck in each direction.

Six Positions on the Torso

1. *Shoulders* – place one hand on the top of each shoulder. You may read that

Back of the head.

Ears and temples.

Eyes.

Throat.

we shouldn't cross the arms over in Reiki, but I have never found this to be a problem. This is a lovely position to use to give yourself Reiki as you fall asleep.

2. *Chest* – place your hands one over the other over your heart.

3. *Stomach* – move your hands down to the stomach.

4. *Kidneys* – move the hands around to the back, either side of the spine.

5. *Coccyx* – move the hands down to either side of the tailbone.

6. *Groin* – move hands around to the groin.

Shoulders.

Shoulders (alternative).

Stomach.

Chest.

Kidneys.

Coccyx.

Two Positions on the Legs

1. *Knees* – place one hand on each knee.

2. *Feet* – either place your hands on the top of each foot, or if that is hard to reach, bring the ankle of one leg onto the knee of the other so that you can hold the top and sole of one foot, and then swap feet.

Knees.

Groin.

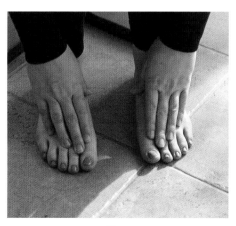

Feet.

Alternative – left foot.

Alternative – right foot.

Once you have your hands in place, all you have to do is think 'Reiki on' and Reiki will start to flow. Work through the hand positions. If at any time you loose your concentration you can just think 'Reiki on' again. If you have Reiki II, then you can add symbols as you feel appropriate either by tracing them onto one or both hands, tracing them over your body or holding the symbol in your mind over your crown chakra and channelling the symbol.

I must warn you that the vast majority of people don't feel Reiki as strongly when they are healing themselves as they do when they are healing others, either in their hands or their bodies. I also find that I don't so naturally fall into the meditative state. Please accept, however, that Reiki is working in you, and if you are patient and keep practising you will start to notice the most remarkable changes in your life.

A Reiki Shower

This is a lovely method of giving yourself a quick Reiki boost and clearing your aura at the same time.

1. Stand comfortably with your feet hip-width apart and make sure you are grounded.

2. Place your hands in the Gassho prayer position and set the intention to give yourself a Reiki shower.

3. Extend your arms above your head with the palms facing down towards your crown chakra and think 'Reiki on'.

4. Keeping your arms extended, move them down in front of your body, keeping your palms turned towards your body. You will probably feel Reiki passing down your body from your hands.

5. While you are moving your arms down they will clear any negative Ki through the aura. Once your hands are opposite your root chakra, turn the palms over to face the ground, and pat all the accumulated negative Ki down to the ground where it is completely neutralized.

6. Return the hands to the Gassho position. You can repeat this exercise twice more.

A REIKI II SELF-HEALING

Because I love the feeling of Reiki, I have searched for a method of self-healing where I could feel the Reiki more noticeably. I have found this method satisfactory, although you do need to be Reiki II and above. I also love that as long at you visualize the Distance symbol, or write it very discreetly in your hand, you can do this self-healing in a public place without anyone realizing!

Sit comfortably with your back straight. Make sure you are grounded, that you have swept your aura clear and that you have your protection in place.

Variation 1 – Draw the Distance symbol and hold the intention to connect to Reiki. Leaving your hands in your lap, visualize going through these hand positions: eyes and third eye; ears and temples; back of the head and a new hand position placing one hand at the hairline above the forehead and the other at the base of your head at the top of the neck.

Variation 2 – Draw the Distance symbol and hold the intention to connect to your higher self. Imagine your higher self getting up, standing behind you and giving you Reiki – you can go through any or all of the hand positions this way.

Variation 3 – Draw the Distance symbol and hold the intention to connect to your higher self. Imagine your higher self sat in front of you and give yourself Reiki. You can actually place the hands just in the air, or keep your hands in your lap imagining that you are placing them. Again you can use any or all hand positions this way.

REIKI AND MEDITATION

Reiki and meditation are beautifully matched, especially as part of self-care, and so it is quite strange that meditation isn't taught as part of most Western-style Reiki classes. I suspect this was another adaptation made by Mrs Takata to make Reiki more palatable in the West. The Japanese style of teaching Reiki does include a number of meditation techniques and most Reiki Master Teachers today do include a number of guided meditations in their classes.

Gassho Meditation

Sensei Usui taught this Gassho meditation ('Gassho' in Japanese means 'hands together'), calling it the First Pillar of Reiki.

All you need is a timer and somewhere comfortable to sit. You want it to be comfortable enough that you don't get any aches or pins and needles, but not so comfortable that you might fall asleep! So this can be the floor if that is comfortable for you, a cushion or a chair. It is preferable to have some part of your body in contact with the floor, so sitting up in bed is not recommended unless this is your only option. If you are sitting in a chair, try to have a cushion at the base of your spine, so that you have to support your back rather than relaxing back into the chair, which again can cause you to fall asleep.

Set your timer for however long you are spending in meditation, then place your hands on your belly. Take two or three slow, deep breaths into your belly, feeling the movement of your hands. Then go back to breathing normally. Now place your hands together in the Gassho or prayer position, with your wrists roughly in front of your heart, your fingertips pointing upwards towards the tip of your nose.

Although it is perfectly possible to meditate with your eyes open, I suggest as a beginner that you meditate with your eyes closed. The visual stimuli can easily cause unwanted thoughts. Then move all your attention (and, if you would like to try the Exercise in Moving Consciousness, your consciousness) to

Gassho meditation.

the point at which your two middle fingers meet. Simply concentrate on this point. If you find any unwanted thoughts coming into your head just let them go – imagine them floating away like a balloon on the breeze – and bring your attention back to the tips of your middle fingers.

Usually with meditation it requires patience to see results. With some people their first experience is very successful, but it may then take many more times before the experience is repeated. My experience was like that. The first time I tried Gassho meditation I found my mind immediately quiet, and I felt myself expand wider and wider. It felt as if the whole Universe fitted inside my head, and that there was still space for more. When

I came out of meditation I found that half an hour had passed in what had seemed in one sense timeless but in another sense only a few moments. Needless to say it took me many more months of practice to be able to repeat the experience, but I was grateful that there was no doubt in my mind what I was aiming for!

Aim to build up to twenty to thirty minutes in this meditation, and if possible repeat it morning and evening. Once your timer goes off, instead of immediately moving, stay in Gassho position and recite the Reiki Principles, either once, or maybe three times.

Just for today...

I will not worry;

I will not anger;

I will give thanks for my many blessings;

I will do my work honestly;

I will show kindness to all living things.

Exercise in Moving Consciousness

I learned this exercise from Jeffrey Allen, a powerful energy healer and teacher. We do not often consider where our consciousness is. Of course we know where our body is, and most of us think of our mind being in our head. If you can learn to move your consciousness it makes it much easier to be fully present and mindful in what you are doing.

I recommend that you read this into a voice recorder so that you can play it back to yourself and follow the exercise.

Start by looking at a place level with your eyes and about 6ft (2m) in front of you. Find a spot that you can focus on – perhaps a mark on the wall. Focus on that spot. Notice when you do so how your consciousness is there in your eyes. Now keeping that awareness in your eyes, close your eyes as gently as you can.

If you have done this successfully you will feel an intensity right behind your eyes. If you don't have that feeling, open your eyes and start again. When you have that intensity behind your eyes move it to one of your ears. You will become intensely aware of your ear – it might even feel as if it moved! Bring the intensity back behind your eyes and then move it to the other ear. Then back behind the eyes again. So I have been calling this a feeling of intensity, but what you are doing is moving your consciousness. Now move your consciousness to the back of your head, and then back to behind your eyes.

You will find with practice that you can move your consciousness to any part of your body, and even outside your body. Practice moving your consciousness to places that are relevant to the task you are doing. So for example move your consciousness to your mouth when you are eating, to your ears when you are listening, to the soles of your feet when you are walking barefoot on sand or grass. Try moving your consciousness to your eyes when you are next talking to someone, or even to your lips when kissing! Be prepared for a strong reaction in the other person – it is very rare that our consciousness is wholly engaged in what we are doing.

To use this technique as part of the Gassho meditation, move your consciousness to the tip of your middle finger. You have a choice either to move your consciousness to your heart, divide it and send out to each shoulder, down to the elbow, wrist, then fingers, or not to divide at the heart and just move down through one arm.

Joshin Kokyu-Ho – The Cleansing Breath

This method is taught in Japanese Reiki classes, and teaches you to consciously channel Reiki, making your energy stronger. You can perform it daily for up to half an hour. *If at any time during this exercise you start to feel dizzy or light-headed, just return to your normal breathing pattern.*

Sit comfortably with your hands in your lap, palms facing upwards. Close your eyes and quieten your mind. Set your intention to perform Joshin Kokyu-Ho, the cleansing breath. Place your hands over your belly with your thumb in line with your navel and fingertips meeting in the middle. Start to bring your attention to your in-breath, consciously expanding your belly so that the hands become further apart as you breathe in, and closer together again as you breathe out.

Now with each in-breath, imagine that you are drawing Reiki in through the crown of your head. With each in-breath Reiki is drawn in through your crown, travels down the hara line, the central line of your body, past each of your chakras,

until it reaches your tanden, which is about two or three finger widths below your navel, under the palms of your hand.

After you have done this for a few breaths, continuing with the same visualization on the in-breath, hold your breath for a few seconds after the in-breath, and in this time visualize Reiki spreading out from your tanden throughout your body.

After you have done this for a few breaths, and continuing with the visualizations on the in-breath and holding the in-breath, now bring your attention to the out-breath, and become aware of Reiki flowing out through the palms of your hands, your fingertips, your feet and perhaps even from your heart, to fill your aura.

Continue with this practice as long as you like.

Meditation on the Reiki Principles

Meditation on the Reiki Principles will have a profound impact on your spiritual development. Sensei Usui called the Principles 'the secret method to invite happiness' and 'the spiritual medicine for all diseases'.

Try meditating on a principle a day, just repeating the principle as a mantra. If you include 'just for today' there are six principles, so this would give you a week of meditations with one day off. Alternatively, meditate on one principle per week. This will give you six weeks of meditation, which will be extremely powerful.

For an interesting variation, try taking a single word from the principles and meditate on that word. Here are a few suggestions as to how that could work.

Just – consider: 'just' what I need; 'just' right; 'just' beautiful; or 'just' enough.

Today – in the evening, meditate on all the wonderful things that happened 'today'. In the morning, meditate on all the wonderful things that will happen 'today'.

I – consider: 'I' am; what (or who) am 'I'; 'I' will; 'I' can; 'I' love; 'I' am loved; 'I' love me; or 'I' am enough.

Anger – repeat as a mantra 'I now let go of my anger' *or* think about the last time you were really angry. Spend some time thinking of all of the bad things that happened as a result of your being angry. Imagine writing down a summary of those things on a piece of paper then screwing up the piece of paper and throwing it away (you can do this in real life rather than your imagination if you like). Then think back to the precise moment just before you got angry. Then imagine what could have happened if you hadn't got angry. Play this forwards in your mind to the present day, and see how different things could have been.

Worry – repeat as a mantra 'I now let go of my worry' *or* try the above exercise substituting worry for anger.

Blessings – this is a gratitude meditation. You could think of three (or five, or ten) things that you are grateful for. For each one, think about why you are grateful, so that you spend at least ten to fifteen seconds on each one, and repeat the words 'thank you, thank you, thank you' before moving on to the next. Or think of a moment that you are grateful for, and for several minutes completely re-live that moment; engage all your senses, see the colours, hear the sounds, notice the fragrances, what could you feel, what could you taste. Re-live all the emotions of joy and happiness; feel your heart beat faster, smile or laugh. Take a deep breath and move those feelings of joy to your heart chakra.

Work – if you love your work, use the exercise above to give thanks for what you do. If you don't love your work, meditate on what you would like to be doing instead.

Meditating on the Symbols (Reiki II)

Meditation on the symbols is a wonderful way to become familiar with what they look like, how to draw them, what their particular 'flavour' of Ki is and how you can use them. Until you are familiar with the symbols you can print them and have them close to you whilst you meditate. Open your eyes to remind yourself of the symbol when you need to.

These are just some suggestions as to how to use the symbols in meditation:

Drawing – draw the symbol in front of you in the air using your hand (rather than pointing), tap the symbol and say its mantra three times (either out loud, or in your head). Continually repeat this process, swap hands when the other gets tired. *(Only use this method if you are alone, or if everyone with you already has Reiki II, as the symbol shape and mantra should be kept private.)*

Channelling – imagine the symbol hanging in the air above your crown chakra. On every in-breath draw the symbol's energy in through the crown of your head.

Chanting – each of the Reiki II symbols has a *kotodama*, a simplified form of its mantra which can be chanted. The sound you make when chanting is much less important than the way the sound vibrates in your body. Start by breathing in, and then on the out-breath chant the kotodama, using any note. Try to time the chant so that you complete the kotodama or mantra in one breath. Notice where you feel the vibration, and on the in-breath breathe into that area noticing the contrasting stillness. Repeat the chant on the next out-breath.

Start each meditation sitting comfortably with your back straight, take a deep breath and close your eyes. During this meditation, notice what the energy feels like, whether it associates with a particular colour, sound, smell or even taste. Notice whether you feel it in a particular part of the body. Feel free to ask the symbol any questions you like, such as how you can use the symbol in healing or in your personal development.

These methods can be used with any Reiki symbol you have been attuned to. You might choose to work just with your favourite of the above methods, or with each of the methods in turn.

Try meditating on just one symbol for a week, or even a month, before moving on to the next symbol.

8

HEALING ANIMALS

Once you have Reiki, you can offer Reiki healing to animals. At Reiki I you can work with your and your friends' pets and with wild animals. To work as an animal healer you will need Reiki II so that you can be properly insured.

THE REIKI PRECEPTS

Consent

It is just as important to get consent from an animal before you give it healing as it is from a human. In the same way that next of kin is not competent to give consent on behalf of another human, whilst you do need consent from the pet's caregiver on one level, it is also necessary to get consent from the animal itself.

In the same way as with humans, you have two choices: either to communicate to the animal's higher self, or to offer the Reiki and see if they accept it. With animals I much prefer the method of switching 'Reiki on' in your hands, and holding the intention of offering it. If the animal accepts the healing then you will start to feel Reiki pulling through your hands. If they don't, you won't.

You will need to be patient the first time that you offer Reiki to an animal. Most animals are much more in touch with Ki than we are, and they will be quite puzzled by your sudden interest in something that, to them, it seems that you have ignored their whole lives. They may even be a bit put out that you think you have anything in this arena that you could offer them – yes, of course, I am talking here about cats! If the first time you ask, the answer is 'no' it is fine for you to keep offering provided you accept their decision to refuse.

Value

If you are insured, then of course you will be able to charge the caregiver for healing that you offer to their animal and that is completely reasonable to cover your time and your expenses. But again, as with next of kin consent, the value should come from the patient, not from another.

So you may be wondering how you get payment, or an exchange of skills, from an animal! If so, step back a moment and think of all the things that your pet has done for you in the last week. The last time that they made you laugh, made you feel loved and worthy. There is really no end to the ways in which animals give to us: they are good company, give us unconditional love, are a comfort; they are teachers, showing us how not to worry, and to live in the moment; they keep us healthy and safe, give us food and clothing; they can even be spiritual teachers in the forms of spirit animals and totems.

In fact there is such an imbalance in what we receive from animals versus what we give them, that in fact I think you could offer every animal you meet as much Reiki as they need and you will still not have balanced the scales! So you are safe to assume that you always have a good exchange of value when you offer healing to an animal.

AURAS AND CHAKRAS

Generally, animals have an aura and chakra system that is fairly similar to humans. The majority of pets, such as dogs, cats, horses and rabbits, have chakras in corresponding places so you can probably guess where they are. Generally it appears that birds don't have a sacral chakra, that reptiles only have root, solar plexus, heart and brow chakras and that fish only have root, solar plexus and brow chakras.

It is not essential to check an animal's chakras before or after a healing, and some animals will make it very difficult for you – either seeing the pendulum as a toy they can swipe at or grab, or not staying still long enough for you to check. But it is nice to check them if you can. If you are able to check them both before and after, this gives a good validation to the caregiver of the success of the healing.

GROUNDING, CLEARING AND PROTECTION

You should ground yourself, clear your aura and make sure you have protection in place, just as you would for a human healing. However, grounding the animal at the end of the healing is much less important. This is because animals are generally more grounded than humans, naturally ground themselves and are less likely to injure themselves if they are not grounded. In fact most animals will fall asleep during their treatment and they will ground themselves naturally when they wake up. This is a happy coincidence, as often it will be the animal that will decide to end the treatment, not you, and so it is often not possible to add on an extra minute or two at the end for grounding.

OFFERING HEALING

Prepare the Space

Most often with animal healing it is better to go to where the animal is, rather than have the animal come to you. This will ensure that the animal is as relaxed as it can be. It also enables you to see the animal in its usual environment, and to note its relationship with any other animals that share its space.

Your safety is an important consideration if you are healing dangerous animals, or animals that have the ability to cause you harm. Reiki can be given through glass tanks, over fences, through hedges and into cages and enclosures. Unless the animal is very close to the boundary you will have much more success if you add the Reiki II Distance symbol if you have it. Of course there is never any danger in offering a distance healing, so if you have Reiki II then do consider that as an option.

It is also important to make sure that the animal feels safe. If it shares its space with another animal that it is nervous of, try and have that other animal removed, or at least kept at a distance, for the time that you are giving healing.

Make sure that the animal's movements are not restricted in any way, and that they can walk away from you if they want to.

Prepare Yourself

Make sure that your clothing is appropriate to the animal and place you are going to be working in. For example, with horses you will need to wear sturdy boots; with dogs be aware that hats can make them nervous, so make sure you are not wearing anything on your head. Remove any jewellery. It is a good idea to keep unscented wipes and hand sanitizer with you so that you can clean your hands if you are working where there are no washing facilities. Make sure you have turned off your phone and that there will be no interruptions.

Unlike human treatments, where you might follow a fairly structured treatment using the twelve hand positions, with animal Reiki you are going to need to be more flexible, more creative and more intuitive. Try to be as calm and relaxed as possible, and do spend as much time as you can centring yourself. If you have time, carry out a Reiki self-healing earlier in the day.

Make sure that you are grounded, that your aura is clear and that you have your protection in place.

Prepare Your Client(s)

This will involve both the animal itself and (unless it's a wild animal) its caregiver too.

For the caregiver, explain what Reiki is and what you will be doing during the treatment. Spend some time before the treatment gathering a detailed case history about the animal and also whatever information you can about the caregiver's lifestyle. (Animals are greatly influenced by their caregivers' behaviours, and you need to be aware of whether the issues you are being asked to treat are the animal's own issues, or a reflection of its caregiver's issues. For example, if the caregiver is clinically depressed and their dog seems lacking in energy and spends all day lying on their bed, it could well be the caregiver's health that needs addressing, before the dog can be helped permanently.)

When first approaching the animal, you need to be aware of their behavioural pattern as a species and respectfully align your behaviour to it. For example, staring a dog straight in the eye would be perceived as threatening, as would picking up a cat without letting it get to know you first. If possible, spend time in the presence of the animal just being. Animals are excellent at picking up people's intentions and emotions, so make sure that you tune into your own emotions and approach the animal feeling calm and relaxed.

Hopefully you can offer Reiki in the patient's usual surroundings, to cause as little disruption as possible. The patient should not be restrained or caged other than so far as is absolutely necessary for your or the patient's safety. Reiki can be given through water, blankets, coats, cones and so on.

During the Treatment

As the animal cannot communicate in a way that most of us understand, make sure all your senses are aware of anything the animal is trying to communicate.

Start by looking carefully at your patient; notice their age, the condition of their fur, skin, scale, hair or feathers. Notice how they move, how they stand,

how their body is aligned. Imagine a perfect vertical and horizontal line and check their alignment against those lines. Are they happy to be touched? Do they smell unusual? Are they eating, are they over- or under-weight?

Also notice their living environment. How appropriate is it, and how is the animal responding to the environment; what is your patient doing, thinking, feeling and experiencing?

Depending upon the animal, it might be possible to dowse the chakras; otherwise you can scan them and their aura with your hands. This is possible even at a relative distance – use the Distance symbol to connect if you have it. Notice whether the aura seems bright and energetic; notice any blockage, breakage or stoppage within the system.

Once you have taken in all this information you can proceed to the actual healing session. First you are just going to offer Reiki, and see if they consent. You can offer Reiki simply with your hands by your sides. You can calmly approach the animal if that is appropriate, or if not use the Reiki II Distance symbol to connect. Hold the intention that the animal is free to accept Reiki or not, and that they can simply take as much or as little of the Reiki as they want at that time. Be patient. It can take up to twenty to thirty minutes for an animal to settle into its first treatment.

Once you can feel the Reiki being pulled through your hands you can proceed to give a full healing. Animals generally do not like people's hands in their auras, so animal Reiki is usually

The length of time you allow for the healing, and how long you hold each hand position, will depend upon the size of the animal, how much healing they need and how much time you have available. For each hand position, anywhere between one to five minutes is fine. If you notice the Reiki in your hand getting less, this is a signal for you to move to the next position. But primarily be led by your patient. If you have Reiki II you can use symbols as you feel led.

If you are healing an animal that is used to being stroked by humans you might like to try giving Reiki whilst stroking, either giving Reiki with one hand and stroking with the other, or simply turning Reiki on in both hands while you stroke.

While you are giving healing, notice your patient's reaction. The animal might begin to sigh, relax, droop and dribble, make gurgling stomach noises and even break wind. They might yawn and become sleepy. However, they may also move around a lot and even walk away. Trust the animal to know how they want the treatment, and don't assume this means that they don't want Reiki. Provided that you are holding the intention that the patient will only receive Reiki if they want it, if they don't want the treatment you will feel the flow of energy stop.

When you feel the flow of energy has stopped, look carefully at the changes in your client. You might notice a lengthening of a curled-up spine, an increased ease of movement, a stretching out of strides. Once you are done, thank the animal and give thanks for Reiki.

Offering Reiki.

either offered from a distance or, if the animal agrees, is hands-on. You will find that you can send Reiki over a distance of 3–6ft (1–2m) with Reiki I; to send for greater distances you will need Reiki II. There are set hand positions that you can follow, but it is very likely that the animal will move around you to get the Reiki where it wants it. If you want to use set hand positions, I suggest you start at the shoulder (one side or both, depending upon what you can reach) and move along or down the body, then if appropriate do the legs. It is not common to use hand positions on the head, but you can if it seems appropriate. Always be aware of the animal's reaction to what you are doing. If they don't like a particular hand position just move on, remember that Reiki goes where it is needed.

If you have noticed issues between the animal you are healing and another animal, then as well as healing either or both animals you can also send Reiki to their relationship. At Reiki I just put Reiki into the air between them when they are a few feet apart. With Reiki II, use the Distance symbol to connect to the relationship and then put in lots of Reiki using the Harmony symbol. I did this with a dog and cat that couldn't be in the same house together and now they are good friends.

After the Treatment

Talk to the caregiver about your patient's reactions. Hopefully they will have noticed the animal relax and enjoy the healing.

Make sure the animal has access to plenty of fresh water.

Advise the caregiver that they may notice some differences in bodily functions as the body starts to work more efficiently following the Reiki.

Occasionally symptoms may briefly get worse. This is the body detoxing following the Reiki; it will not last long. If the patient is under the care of a vet, advise the caregiver to have a check-up with the vet soon after the healing, but to continue any medication until the vet advises otherwise.

With most conditions one treatment will not be enough. Usually there will be an immediate improvement; the animal will appear calmer and more relaxed. However you will probably find that things will return to normal unless another healing is given fairly soon. Anything from three to ten healing sessions are usually needed. Ideally the treatments should be quite close together, so if you are healing your own pet feel free to offer two or three healings a day. If this is not possible then try to offer at least three healings within the space of a week.

If this was a paid-for Reiki II healing, complete a client record. (A template client record is set out at Appendix B.)

HEALING CATS

Cats are by their nature independent, and will only accept Reiki from you if they know that they are in control. So be sure to keep the intention that they only receive as much Reiki as they would like. Cats are less likely to approach you, and it's rarely appropriate go straight up to a cat and give it Reiki, so often a distance healing is more acceptable, at least at the start. If you only have Reiki level 1 then you need to keep the distance to around 6ft (2m). Most likely the cat will be able

to sense your Reiki boundary better than you, and will go and sit right at it to receive their healing! As cats often adopt a fairly relaxed posture it might be hard to tell by their behaviour whether they are receiving the Reiki, so keep awareness of the energy flowing through your hands.

If the cat does approach you, then it is of course fine to offer a hands-on healing. Depending upon the size of the cat you will only need a few hand positions. If the cat is lying with its front and back paws tucked in under itself then you can start with hands either side of the spine on the shoulders. You can then move back along the spine, but bearing in mind not all cats like being touched very far back. As Reiki will always go where it is needed there is never a need to use a hand position that the animal doesn't appreciate. If the cat is curled up, then I like to put one hand at the top and one hand at the bottom of the spine. If the cat is lying on its back then I will usually try to slide a hand underneath, one under the head and one under the shoulder.

If there is more than one cat, it is possible to offering healing to more than one at a time. For distance healing, simply sit somewhere between them and turn your palms upward to offer Reiki. If one of the cats would like hands-on, then you can use one hand on that one and offer to the others with the other hand. If two cats want hands-on, you can put a hand on each.

Unless a cat is old or quite ill it will probably only need ten to fifteen minutes of Reiki. If you are healing more than one cat at a time, the healing time will increase.

HEALING DOGS

Dogs are very likely to approach you for a sniff and a stroke and this is a great way to get acquainted. Once you are ready to start, turn your palms up and start to offer Reiki. They will probably have another sniff, and then hopefully find a comfortable position to settle into to receive healing. If they settle within reach, then by all means try hands-on. If they settle a short distance away then you can offer distance healing up to about 6ft (2m). Anything beyond that and you will need to use the Reiki II Distance symbol to connect.

Again, with dogs I like to start at the shoulder, either side of the spine if the dog is sitting or lying flat on its tummy; if it is lying on its side then start with one hand on the shoulder and the other on the hip. For an emotional healing, you can reach the heart chakra by putting one hand on the chest and the other at the top of the shoulder with the dog either sitting or lying on its side. Make sure that you move around your animal; don't expect the animal to position itself the way you might prefer. But also be aware that the dog may move around you to receive healing where they want it!

Depending upon the size, age and fitness of the dog they may need anything from ten to forty minutes of Reiki.

Emotional healing on the heart chakra.

Physical healing on the body.

Let the animal show you where they need healing.

HEALING HORSES

You can treat horses in a stable or in the field. Reiki will penetrate through fly-guards, bandages, blankets and so on; there is no need to remove anything. If the horse is saddled, then I would have it removed for their comfort except if you are in a first aid situation where you should interfere as little as possible.

Make sure that you are wearing sturdy boots in case the horse treads on your foot by accident. I do sometimes have the caregiver hold a horse on a halter, especially if I don't know the horse, and/or it is quite windy or the horse is in any way unsettled. This is just to steady the horse for my safety. But I always instruct the caregiver to allow the horse to move calmly any way that it wants to.

If you are working in a stable, then approach and greet the horse in the normal way without using Reiki, so with a few soft words and a gentle pat. Unless this is your horse, *never* offer a patient food. You are here to offer healing; you do not want to confuse matters by having the animal approach you for food. Once you have greeted the horse you can start to offer Reiki. Offer it with your hands down by your sides so as not to look threatening. When you feel Reiki starting to flow, you know the horse has consented and you can proceed with the treatment.

If you are in a field, then unless you fancy a long walk, you might want to start offering Reiki from the gate, especially if you have the Reiki II Distance symbol. If the horse is interested it will probably start walking towards you. Again, start to offer Reiki with your hands down by your sides. If you have the Reiki II Distance symbol you can proceed with the treatment once you feel Reiki flowing. If you only have Reiki I you will need to walk towards the horse until you are no more than 6ft (2m) away.

Once the horse accepts the healing, it is likely that you will notice some dramatic changes in behaviour. The horse will probably stop eating, and its head may droop. There are usually some very dramatic tummy rumbles! This all shows that the Reiki is being accepted. You can work at a distance, or hands-on working through the set hand positions or following your intuition. If you need to walk behind the horse take care to make it very clear what you are doing so that you don't get kicked; either be a good distance away or very close and in contact with the horse so that the horse knows you are there.

If the horse is not alone in the field, and one of the other horses is more dominant, you will probably find the dominant horse muscling in on the treatment. You can create an energetic barrier between you and the dominant horse, effectively blocking the flow of energy so that it will lose interest and hopefully walk away. Do this by swiping your arm down three times where you want the barrier and with the intention of creating it. Alternatively you can try offering healing to the dominant horse first until he has had enough. Be warned though, some horses never have enough! If possible, have your patient alone in a fenced-off part of the field.

Hand Positions for a Horse

For any medium-size horse, I usually use eight positions on the body (four each side), and four positions on each leg. I rarely treat a horse's head. Imagine the length of the body divided into four. Then place one hand at the top of the shoulder below the spine, and the other next to it so you are covering about half the length. The next hand position will be to move along the back to the rear half, your furthest hand being quite high on the rump. Then move back to the front, and repeat the hand positions, but lower down. For a pony, or smaller or larger horse, simply have your hands closer together or further apart.

You can then move on down to the legs on that side before moving to the next side, or if you prefer you can do the other side of the body and then do all the legs at the end. When doing the legs, squat to the side so that you can move away quickly if the horse wants to move. If there are a lot of flies and the horse is stamping, you may prefer not to do the hand positions on the legs. In this case, spend more time at the top of each leg and trust Reiki to flow down the leg to where it is needed. If you have the opportunity, you can hold the intention to send grounding at the end of the healing, but if by this time the horse has had enough it is fine not to specifically ground.

Top shoulder and back.

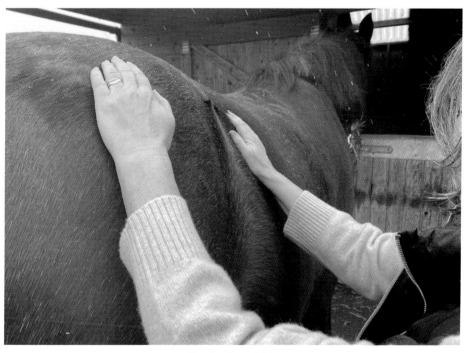

Top back and hip.

Lower shoulder and barrel.

Lower flank and thigh.

Thigh.

Knee.

Fetlock and hoof.

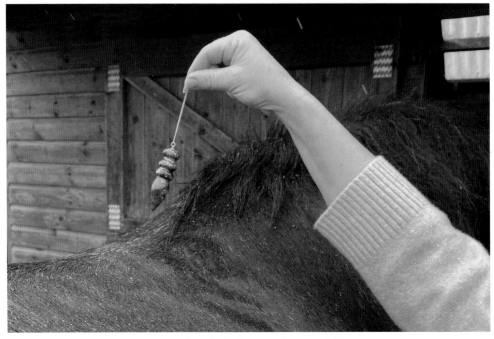

Testing Flynn's chakras with a pendulum.

Horses will usually take a surprising amount of Reiki, especially older horses who are prone to arthritis. For a full healing, allow a good hour.

The horse will usually make it quite clear when the healing is over, giving you a good nudge with its nose to say thank you.

HEALING SMALL ANIMALS

It might seem that holding a small animal in your cupped hands is the obvious way to give it Reiki, but the heat of Reiki can be too much for very small animals. If a mouse, hamster, gerbil or similar animal will settle on one hand then you can give it Reiki that way. Alternatively you can give it Reiki whilst it is in its cage. Take

care here to keep the intention that the animal will only receive so much Reiki as it wants to receive, as it will not be able to move away.

If you have Reiki II you can use distance healing to send Reiki whilst the patient is free to roam around the room.

HEALING AQUATICS

Animals that live in water can be treated without taking them out of their tank, or whatever water they live in. Water has a memory, and has a magnifying effect on Reiki, so start by giving Reiki with your hands a short distance from the tank or surface of the water. After the first few treatments the patient will be used to the

Reiki and you can start to put your hand on the tank or even in the water.

As the water conducts Reiki, you will find that giving Reiki to one fish in a tank or pond will in fact give Reiki to all life forms in the water. Just be aware that this might have an impact on the growth of weed and algae in the water.

TREATING DANGEROUS OR CAGED ANIMALS

When dealing with a wild, poisonous, angry or anxious animal it is wise to use a distant treatment. If you are a Reiki level I healer you need to be in the presence of the animal, at a safe distance, but no more than 6ft (2m) away. At Reiki II you can use distance healing. Whatever

the distance, Reiki will go through glass, fences, and cages, so you can keep a safety barrier between you and the animal.

If the animal is in a small space, take care to notice when it has had sufficient Reiki as it will be unable to move away from you.

ANIMALS WHO REFUSE REIKI

You may occasionally come across an animal who for whatever reason does not want to accept Reiki. You cannot

and should not force an animal to receive Reiki. But you can always send Reiki into a situation. Here use the information that you gained studying the animal, its environment and its relationships and identify anything that might be contributing to the animal's situation. For example, perhaps there is an unpleasant atmosphere where the animal lives – you can clear it energetically by smudging or with Reiki and give Reiki to the room or cage. Or perhaps the animal has an unhealthy relationship with another house guest, in which case you can send Reiki to their relationship. (The relationship is separate from the animals in the relationship, so you don't need consent to send Reiki to a relationship.)

If you feel that the animal would accept Reiki but is fearful of you, you could Reiki their bedding, water and toys. But do not use this as a covert attempt to give them Reiki; make sure you hold the intention that they will only absorb as much Reiki from these things as they want.

PESTS

Despite the Reiki Principle 'Show Kindness to All Living Things' there are some animals that we just don't want to live too close to. For example, you can't really allow rodents to live in your house as they chew electric cable, and spiders in the house make cobwebs that make the place look dirty.

You can use Reiki to assist in the communication with insects and rodents, to set the rules by which we can live alongside each other. It is not kind to just banish these animals altogether, so try to include a positive suggestion as to where else they can live undisturbed.

Co-Existing with Pests

Try these methods to communicate with animals:

- Turn 'Reiki on' and trace a line of Reiki light with the fingers of one hand for insects trapped in your room to guide them to the window. You usually need to trace the line three times.

- If you feel the need to put traps down, give rodents time to find another home first, perhaps in an outbuilding. Whilst offering Reiki, talk in your mind to the animal's higher self. Tell them what the problem is and offer them a solution. I usually give them three days' warning to find another home.

- To keep your vegetable patch free of 'pest' damage, dedicate one row in your vegetable patch for caterpillars, slugs and snails to snack from. Again, offer Reiki whilst telling them where they can eat.

9

HEALING THE PLANET

The beautiful planet on which we are so privileged to live has supported us for over 50,000 years. It is time that we gave some healing back. I add a healing to the planet into each of my Reiki shares. You can, of course, simply put your hands on the ground and think 'Reiki on', but here are a few other ideas you can try:

- Send healing using a globe, simply placing your hands upon it and turning 'Reiki on'. You can use your intention and placement of the hands to send healing to the planet generally or to a particular area(s).

- You can use a picture of the planet, or an atlas, either holding the picture in

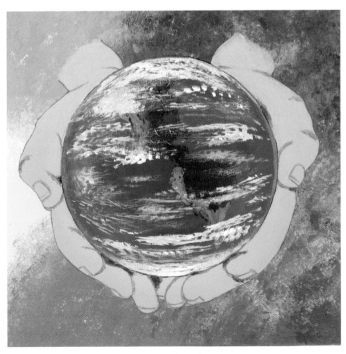

Healing the planet.

your hands or placing your hands on the page and turning 'Reiki on'. Try the same thing with the wonderful illustration at the beginning of the chapter.

- If you are a visual person, you might like to create a ball of Reiki to heal the planet as a whole. Once you have created the ball of Reiki, imagine the planet shrinking down so that it fits into your Reiki ball. Watch the Earth revolving slowly, absorbing the Reiki. When you have finished, imagine shrinking the ball of Reiki so that it fits entirely within the planet, and imagine the planet back at its proper place and size in the Universe. Intend that the ball of Ki now at the core of the Earth can be tapped into to give Reiki to all those who are in need of healing, including the planet itself.

- We usually talk about giving Reiki through our hands, but it is equally possible to send Reiki with our feet. So a very tactile and easy way to send healing to the planet is to simply sit with your feet flat on the ground and turn 'Reiki on'.

- Why not try the above as part of a walking meditation, giving healing to the planet with each step that you take. If you have Reiki II, try walking the shape of the Power symbol as a form of walking meditation whilst giving healing to the planet.

- William Rand of the International Centre for Reiki Training has placed a crystal grid at each of the poles and in Jerusalem. The grids are made of copper and clear quartz crystals, and contain the inscription, 'May the followers of all religions and spiritual paths work together to create peace among all people on Earth'. They are designed to receive Reiki from anyone who sends it and to distribute the Reiki around the world to promote peace. So another option in healing the planet is to send Reiki to one of these grids. Simply place your hands on the picture of the grid and turn 'Reiki on'. You can download cards that contain pictures of the grids from the International Centre for Reiki Training.

Whilst sending healing to the planet generally you could also spend a couple of moments offering Reiki to:

- All people on the planet.

- All animals on the planet.

- All plants on the planet.

World Peace card.

Create a Ball of Reiki

To create a ball of Reiki, first make sure that you are grounded, that your aura is clear and that you have your protection in place. Hold your hands out just in front of you, palms facing each other and turn 'Reiki on'. Intend that the Reiki flows from both palms and where the two beams meet they form a ball of healing energy. As you continue to channel Reiki, allow your hands to spread further apart so that the ball of Reiki can grow bigger.

If you have friends that are attuned to Reiki you can do the same thing by all standing in a circle and beaming Reiki into the middle. I have even used this technique very successfully with a group of people all on video conference, just imagining ourselves in a healing circle and beaming Reiki into the middle.

Once you have your ball of Reiki you can invite people, things or situations into it for healing, or you can put the ball over something that needs healing. Try putting the ball on top of your head and allowing it to flow down over yourself.

- The water and air that support all life.

- The rocks and minerals that make up the planet.

As you are simply offering Reiki here you do not need to get consent.

Whichever method you use, try not to focus on the negative pictures carried by most news services. Always imagine the Earth or the location completely healed – a place of joy, peace and unconditional love.

HEALING PLANTS

As well as including all plant life in a planetary healing, you can offer Reiki to individual plants.

Reiki seeds before you plant them by holding the packet between your hands.

Once seeds are planted, and for plants in pots, you can hold your hands either side of the pot and offer Reiki. For a fun experiment with children, plant up two pots of seeds and give Reiki to one of the pots every day but not the other. See how much faster and stronger the plants that received Reiki grow.

For bigger plants, you can send Reiki to the leaves, and for trees you can send to the trunk.

Once rooted, plants don't need grounding.

10

OTHER USES OF REIKI

USING REIKI AT WORK

Whether you are in a job that you love, where you hope to thrive, or in a job that you hate and just need to survive, using Reiki at work can help.

Protection

If you work in a challenging environment with people you don't trust or where you feel undermined or even threatened (obviously here I don't mean where you feel physically threatened or mentally abused; in those cases you should immediately get help from Human Resources or the police if appropriate), you can use Reiki to protect yourself, your workspace and your work product. Imagine wrapping yourself, your office or whatever you want to protect in a bubble of protection. Set the rule in your mind that only energy that serves your highest and greatest good can get through the bubble. If you have Reiki II, use the Power symbol instead of the bubble.

Creating a Positive Environment

You can also use Reiki to create a positive environment in which to work. Give Reiki to the walls, desk, chair or whatever else is present where you want to create the positive atmosphere. When I worked as a lawyer I wanted to make sure that I knew what was going on in the company that I worked for. I used to Reiki my office every morning, making it feel positive and welcoming, with a result that people would often gravitate to my office and discuss what they were working on. If you have Reiki II, trace either or both the Power and Harmony symbols into the middle of the space and leave it there (you will need to re-trace the symbol daily).

Grounding

When you are grounded you are present in the moment, and very aware of what is happening around you. Being grounded in a busy environment can sometimes feel like time has slowed down, giving you time to observe and react appropriately. Refer back to Chapter 5 for further details of how to ground yourself. As well as grounding yourself you can ground other people, animals, things and even situations. You do not need consent to do this, as being grounded is a natural state.

Phone Calls and Meetings

Send Reiki into phone calls and video conferences to make them more collaborative and to reduce conflict. Be clear that you are sending Reiki to the call or meeting, not to the individuals involved (for which you would need their consent). Simply by touching the phone or computer and thinking 'Reiki on' you can send Reiki into a phone or video conversation.

REIKI FOR PERSONAL DEVELOPMENT

In the West we usually think of Reiki as a tool for healing. However in Japan, where Reiki originated, it was a path to spiritual enlightenment, and the ability to use Reiki to heal was a pleasant side effect. So Reiki is an important tool in spiritual development, but can also be used in other areas of personal development such as breaking bad habits, setting new habits or goals, and manifestation.

The Reiki Principle 'Just for today... I will do my work honestly', can amongst other things be interpreted as a requirement to work on your own self-development, and it is true that anything that you are trying to do will be done more easily, faster and with more joy if it is done with Reiki. I have used Reiki to help clients buy the house of their dreams, get a job that is perfect for them, learn a language and learn to play a musical instrument. Reiki will also help with the little things, like finding a car parking space, your keys or deciding what to wear.

Goal Setting

It is not a surprise that Reiki and goal setting work so well together, as the Reiki Principles are behavioural goals. I don't actually work with the Reiki Principles in the same way that I work with more task-oriented goals. (For more on working with the Reiki Principles, *see* Chapter 6, Healing Yourself.)

For task-related goals I usually set three or four big goals for the year. An example might be 'to build a thriving Reiki practice', or 'to learn a new language'. To make these more manageable, I break these down into quarterly goals, such as 'find a treatment room' or 'find a language tutor'. I break these down further into monthly goals such as 'design business cards' or 'spend an hour a day learning vocabulary'. You can, of course, go down to weekly goal detail if that is helpful for you.

Once you have created your goals, write a record card for each goal. Write your goal in as much detail as you can, including the date or time by which it needs to be done, and at the bottom of the card write 'this, or better than this please'. You can then take each card between your hands and turn 'Reiki on'. Send Reiki for as much time as you can, as often as you can. For bigger goals, up to twenty minutes per day works wonders. For smaller goals you can spend less time. Remember that any amount of Reiki is better than none. When you have achieved your goal write 'thank you, thank you, thank you' across the card. I like to keep all my old cards to remind me of what I have achieved!

If you have Reiki II then you can add symbols to make this process more powerful. Use the Distance symbol to connect to the time in the future when you want to have completed your goal, then trace first the Harmony symbol to create the mental and emotional energy necessary to achieve your goal, and then the Power symbol to power the other symbols and to empower the goal. You can just trace the symbols with your finger, but if you choose to draw the symbols in pen or pencil you will need to burn the card when you have finished using it.

Releasing Limiting Beliefs

We all have limiting beliefs. A limiting belief is a belief that we hold as being true, and therefore act in accordance with, but which is not actually true. These beliefs hold us back from reaching our full potential.

To test whether a belief that you hold is a limiting belief or not, consider whether the belief is true for everyone. If it is (for example, 'I can't fly [without a wing of some sort]') then you can safely assume that it is not a limiting belief, it is a truth. If it is not true for everyone (for example, 'it's not possible to make a good living from working with Reiki') then that is a limiting belief.

We usually create limiting beliefs when we are quite young, and accordingly most limiting beliefs come from our family or 'tribe'. We form them to help with our survival and our acceptance by the rest of the pack. They are often core beliefs and derive from religion or societal rules. However, as each generation strives to improve on the generation before, we need to challenge these beliefs and consider if they are beliefs that we are happy to continue to choose to live by.

A great demonstration of limiting beliefs at work was the four-minute mile. There was a time when it was thought impossible for a human to run a mile in four minutes; in fact it was referred to as the 'four-minute mile barrier'. When Roger Bannister achieved the four-minute mile in 1954 it proved that the barrier was a limiting belief, not a fact. Since then, nearly 1,500 runners have achieved the four-minute mile.

Once you have identified a limiting belief that you no longer want to live with, you can dispel it using the Circle of Eight technique (described in Chapter 12, Advanced Healing Techniques) and/or Seiheki Chiryo method below. For the Circle of Eight, simply put the limiting belief itself into the other circle and follow

Common Limiting Beliefs

'There are never enough hours in a day to get everything done'

'I will never be financially secure'

'I'm no good with numbers'

'I am not worthy of love'

'I will never find true love'

'Good things never happen to me'

'I am not capable of earning more than [£60,000] per year'

the script. Ideally, use the technique every day for a week, or longer if you feel necessary. For Seiheki Chiryo you will need to create an affirmation that is the opposite to your limiting belief. For example, for the limiting belief 'It's impossible to make a living from Reiki' your affirmation might be 'Lots of people make a good living from Reiki and I'm so happy that I can too'. Use the affirmation in performing the method, and try to carry out the method two or three times a day for at least a week.

Using Reiki to Break Bad Habits and Create Good Habits – Seiheki Chiryo

This technique can be used either on yourself or on someone else to de-programme bad habits and instil new good habits.

First you need to decide on an appropriate affirmation. Make sure that the affirmation is in ordinary, simple language. If you are working with someone else, agree the affirmation with them using language they are comfortable with and write it down.

Stand sideways – on to your patient so that the hand that you usually write with is at the back of your client, and the other is at the front. Make sure that you are grounded, clear your aura and put your protection in place. If you have Reiki II, draw the Power symbol over the hand that is at the back, and the Harmony symbol over the hand that is at the front. Working 'hands-off', place one hand at the back of the patient's head and the other at the forehead and allow Reiki to flow. Send Reiki for two or three minutes, reciting the affirmation in your mind, holding the intention of drawing out the bad habit and replacing it with the good intention of the affirmation.

Creating Affirmations

An affirmation is a positive statement that is used to dispel negativity and to instil positive thinking. Some people find them hard to write because whilst they are a statement of something that we wish to be true, in the here and now they are not actually true. However, the negative thinking that we use them to replace isn't really true either. For example, there is no more truth in the thought 'This dead-end job is killing me' than there is in the affirmation 'I am enjoying a challenging and rewarding career'.

When you are writing an affirmation make sure it:

- Is positive.
- Is precise.
- Is in the present tense ('I am...' not 'I will...').
- Is personal (usually it will start with 'I am...').
- Includes positive emotion (this is how we communicate with the Universe).

Here are some examples:

'I am happy' 'I am a magnet for positive energy' 'I am enough' 'I love exercise' 'I enjoy healthy eating'

Seiheki Chiryo if you are right-handed.

Seiheki Chiryo if you are left-handed.

After two or three minutes, remove the hand from the forehead and stop reciting the affirmation. Allow Reiki to continue to flow to the back of the head for a few more minutes.

Give your client a copy of the affirmation and ask them to repeat it three times every morning and night for twenty-eight days.

Using Reiki to Help Learn

Whether you are studying for exams, learning new skills for your job or simply learning for the fun of it, Reiki can help in a number of ways. It can help you help yourself or others.

The need to learn, whether there is an exam at the end or not, can cause stress and anxiety, and these are the least helpful states for learning. A normal Reiki healing concentrating on the head and the feet will help reduce and even remove feelings of stress and anxiety. While you are giving Reiki, calmly visualize the exam going very well, with all the right questions, finishing within the time limit and so on. Continue the visualization into the future to results day and visualize receiving the hoped-for results.

Hand positions to work on are the third eye to enhance memory and recall, and temples and back of the head for brain function. For a subject that is part logical and part creative, if you have Reiki II, use the Harmony symbol over the temples to balance left and right brain function.

If you are comfortable starting to work more psychically, you can use Reiki to access the Akashic Records. The Akashic Records is a library of all thoughts, words, deeds and emotions that have ever been or ever will be. You can use the Distance symbol to access and interrogate the Akashic Records.

Sending Reiki to Future Events (Reiki II)

If you have Reiki II, use the Distance symbol to connect you to the time and place of any future event and send both the Harmony and Power symbols to help with stress, anxiety and performance on the day. You can do this for yourself or for someone else. You can do this for exams, the driving test, interviews, public speaking engagements, performances, anything where Reiki can help you perform to the best of your ability, and where it might be difficult to give Reiki at the time.

USING REIKI IN MANIFESTATION

Manifestation, the Law of Attraction and the concept of Abundance are all very popular at the moment, with many films, books and courses devoted to the practice. Although not taught in mainstream education, it is an essential life skill, necessary if we are to live as full a life as possible.

Most people mistakenly think that because the concept behind manifestation is simple, that the practice is simple too. They have a couple of half-hearted attempts at manifesting a few things and then become despondent when they are not successful. On the other hand, there are a few that truly grasp the concept.

They succeed in re-training their minds and their ways of thinking to enable them to succeed.

We are very fortunate then to be able to use Reiki to enhance our ability to manifest.

Manifestation is a three-step process: first we have to be able to imagine what it is that we want, then we have to communicate to the Universe that we want it, then we have to be grateful that we have received it. You might think that two of these steps come before we receive and the third comes afterwards, but this is the thinking that causes most people to fail in manifestation. It is crucial that we carry out all three steps before we receive.

Imagine What it is that You Want

We create through our thoughts. Every single thing that we do is a thought before it is a deed. Even before we mindlessly brush our teeth in the morning our minds must tell our bodies to pick up the toothbrush. Manifestation is no different. The word 'imagine' gives us a clue of the best way to do this, and that is to form an image of what it is that you want. You can simply form an image in your mind, and for the many thousands of simple things that we make happen in a day this is sufficient. But if we are thinking about manifestation it is usually because we have something quite dramatic in mind, something that is different from that which we already have. For this we need to put in a bit more effort.

If you are a naturally visual person you may be able to simply close your eyes and imagine what it is that you want.

You might imagine yourself on holiday, or receiving a large cheque in the post, or buying a new house. Fill your visualization with colour, and include as many of the other senses as you can, adding sounds, smells, tastes and sensations. Make it as real as possible.

If you find it hard to visualize then you might need to do something more tangible than visualizing what you want. If you are good with words you might want to write down a description of what you want; you could use a record card to write down the details. Make sure that the language is concise, positive and expressed in the present tense. Be careful of the language that you use. We often make the mistake of asking (in prayer or otherwise) for what we want; 'I want to be well' 'I want a new car'. But the word 'want' not only describes a thing that we desire, but also our current lack of it, for example 'you shall *want* for nothing'. If we communicate our 'want' to the Universe then to be 'wanting' or 'lacking' is what the Universe understands your desire to be. Equally, if your desire is stated in the future tense, 'I am looking forward to my new car' – the Universe thinks your desire is to be in anticipation, and so you will always be looking forward to it, never actually receiving it. Instead you need to make your language positive and as if what you desire has already happened: 'I am so happy that I am well'; 'I love my new car'. For some people this might feel like a lie, but it didn't feel like a lie when you were just visualizing, so try to apply that same logic. You are just describing what it is that you desire in language that the Universe can understand.

For something big, you might create a vision board combining pictures clipped from magazines, photos, words, fabrics and small items that relate to what you desire. You can even create a virtual vision board, cutting and pasting images combined with text boxes.

Whichever method you use to create your image you must be certain to include *who* you want this to happen to (so include a photo of the person, and/or write their name in any text) and the date or rough time frame in which you want it to happen (again, write the date, or clip in a section of a calendar). So for example, if you want a holiday of a lifetime for yourself and your partner, in your imaging/imagining be sure to include yourself and your partner at your dream location on a certain date.

Communicate to the Universe

The language of the Universe is emotion; how we feel about something. Instead of communicating our feeling of lack of what we want, we need to communicate our joy in having the thing even before we receive it. Greg Braden tells a wonderful story of an American Indian living in New Mexico. There had been long drought, and the American Indian invited Greg to walk with him into the desert to ask for rain. Greg imagined the man was going to perform some kind of rain dance or other ritual, but after he had been stood there completely still for a short while the man said that he had done what needed to be done and they could leave. When Greg asked what it was that he had done he said that he had

imagined himself feeling the joy he would feel if it was actually raining. Needless to say, a couple of days later the rains came. So it is by showing the Universe through our emotions how happy we will feel when we receive what we desire that we communicate to the Universe what it is that we desire.

This is the most difficult step in the process, but we can use Reiki to help. Depending upon the size of your record card or vision board you can either hold it between your cupped hands, or prop it up in front of you like a picture in a frame, and then send Reiki. At Reiki I, have the palms of your hands in contact with, or very close to, the note or board, and simply think 'Reiki on'. At Reiki II and above you have the option to beam Reiki to the item, and to use whichever symbol(s) seems most appropriate to you; use the Distance symbol to connect to the time that you want this to happen, and the Power symbol to power your desire. Add the Harmony symbol for any emotional or relationship matters.

Now whilst you are giving Reiki consider how you will feel when you receive this thing that you desire. Engage all of your senses, picturing yourself receiving what you desire, imagine who is with you, where you are; fill the image with colour. What can you hear in this vision, what noises are far away, what sounds can you hear in the mid-distance, and what can you hear close to you? Are there any fragrances or flavours associated with what you desire? If so imagine that you can smell or taste them. If it is your desire to travel to Italy, imagine that you can smell oregano on the air, a pizza cooking in an outdoor oven; imagine taking a bite of the pizza, the crisp base, the sharp taste of tomato, the melted cheese running down your chin. What can you feel? The temperature of the air on your skin, the texture of what you are wearing. In your imagination reach out and touch something – what does it feel like?

While you are doing all this imagining, notice how you feel. You should be feeling exactly how you will feel when you receive the thing that you desire. Perhaps your heart is beating faster with excitement, you might find yourself smiling, you are probably experiencing pure joy. This is the way that you communicate to the Universe what it is that you want. Become extremely aware of how you feel while you continue to send Reiki. If you have Reiki II, use the Distance symbol now to send these pure feelings of joy and

Sample Visualizations

A new partner – write down in detail all the attributes that you are looking for in a person; where they live, what they do, their character, their situation. Write down everything that is important to you. If you are artistic you can draw a picture (this should not be someone that you already know). When you send Reiki to the words or picture, imagine a place and circumstance where you might meet. Hear the sounds in that place, see the surroundings in full colour, notice the smells. You might even imagine the first words you say to each other, the first touch. Feel that buzz of excitement. Communicate this positive feeling to the Universe.

Money – write down the amount of money that you need. Imagine being in your house, and hearing the sound of the letterbox. An envelope falls to the floor. Imagine picking up the envelope, feel the paper in your hands. Imagine tearing open the envelope – or perhaps you use a letter-opener – and pulling out a cheque made payable to you for the exact amount of money

that you need. Or imagine yourself walking outside in the woods. It's a beautiful day, birds are singing and the sun is shining through the trees. You feel a gentle breeze against your skin and blowing through your hair. Each time the breeze blows through the trees money falls down around you. You bend down and pick up what you need. Who said money doesn't grow on trees?! Feel happy that you have received what you need and communicate your happiness to the Universe.

Holiday – create a vision board with pictures of your desired destination, a mocked-up travel ticket, a photo of yourself and whoever else you want to go with you and the date you want to go. Whilst sending Reiki to the board, imagine yourself waking up on the morning you are going on holiday, packing a last few items in your bag or suitcase and travelling to your destination. Imagine the views, the flavours, smells and sounds of your destination. Feel the excitement and communicate it to the Universe.

love to the Universe. Do this for as much time as you can spare each day. Just before you finish, mentally store away this feeling so that whenever you find yourself thinking about the thing that you desire during the day, you can spend a few moments experiencing the joy again. Make sure that you are holding these feelings of positive love and joy more often than you are feeling the lack of what you want.

Express Gratitude

To dispel the feelings of lack, and to continue to communicate effectively to the Universe, you need to feel grateful for what you have received, even before you receive it.

One of the Reiki Principles is '*just for today... I will give thanks for my many blessings*'. So as part of your daily Reiki practice, when you recite the Reiki Principles, literally list your desires and give thanks that the Universe is in the process of giving you what you desire.

Don't try to use Reiki or the Law of Manifestation to make somebody else do something that they don't want to do. For example, whilst you can use Reiki to manifest a new partner, in which case Reiki will bring you your perfect partner who may or may not be someone that you already know, you cannot use Reiki to make a certain person fall in love with you, as that may not be in their best interests.

USING REIKI WITH CRYSTALS

Reiki and crystals are mutually beneficial. You can use Reiki to cleanse and charge crystals, and crystals also enhance Reiki.

To use Reiki to help you choose a crystal to buy or to work with, switch 'Reiki on' and sweep your hand over the crystals with the intention to identify which crystal is appropriate. You will find that your hand becomes hotter or tingles when it is over the right crystal.

Once you have chosen your crystal, it needs to be cleansed. Crystals absorb negative Ki and this must be cleared for the crystal to work most effectively. As long as you know that your crystal is not water soluble you can cleanse it in running water. Or you can bury a crystal in earth or salt for a couple of days. Alternatively, give the crystal Reiki with

the intention that it is cleansed. Hold the crystal in your hands and turn 'Reiki on'. Reiki will turn off automatically when the cleansing is done. If you have Reiki II, use the Harmony symbol to cleanse.

After cleansing it is a good idea to charge your crystal. You can do this by putting it out in moonlight, placing it with other crystals (particularly with a carnelian) or you can give it Reiki. Hold the crystal in your hands and turn 'Reiki on' intending to power the crystal. Again Reiki will turn off automatically when the crystal is sufficiently charged.

Crystals that are used in healing need to be cleansed between each healing. Otherwise consider using the phases of the moon to remind you to cleanse and charge your crystals every month on the full moon.

11

THE REIKI SYMBOLS

On the twenty-first day of his fasting and meditation on Mount Kurama, at the moment he received enlightenment, Sensei Usui saw the symbols that he had discovered in the Sanskrit scrolls coming towards him as pure light out of the sky. We now know these as the Reiki symbols, however they were not incorporated into the teaching of Reiki until after Sensei started working with Chujiro Hayashi and the other naval officers.

In Japan Reiki was, and to a large extent is still today, seen as a system for achieving enlightenment. The ability to use Reiki to heal others is a side-effect experienced along the way to enlightenment rather than the purpose of learning Reiki, as it tends to be in the West. This was reflected in the character of Usui's students. His students were devoted to their spiritual development, on a journey that was one of slow, steady progress, each student spending hours each day in meditation and self-healing. Their lessons would be weekly, and many, many months or even years could be spent on each level as the Ki, and the students' sensitivity to and awareness of it, developed.

This was not the case for the naval officers, who were not spiritual men. They wanted to be able to learn to use Reiki in healing quickly and easily, so in teaching the naval officers Usui introduced the symbols. The symbols are in effect a shortcut, providing quick and easy access to profound spiritual energy, and they enable Reiki to be learned by anyone.

I hope that this helps to explain why it is that, until 1992,[8] the symbols had been kept secret by all those receiving Reiki; and why, even now that the symbols are readily available in books and on the internet, we should treat the symbols with respect, as sacred tools. This is also the reason why I have chosen not to include the shape or mantra of the symbols in this book. I have already said that it is necessary for you to learn direct from a Reiki Master Teacher; this teacher will teach you how to draw the symbols and speak their mantras.

When Mrs Takata taught Reiki II her students would not have seen the symbols before class, would have spent most of the class learning the symbols, and when leaving class were not allowed to take any written record of the symbols with them. As people's memories are not perfect, this perhaps explains why we sometimes see the symbols drawn slightly differently. Mrs Takata did leave one written record of the symbols; these are the versions that I was taught, and that I both teach and use in healing. However, whichever version you are taught and attuned to will be the right version for you.

It is incumbent on us as Reiki students to learn to use the symbols correctly, to draw them accurately and to remember their mantras.

DRAWING THE SYMBOLS

Many times in this book I have referred to 'drawing' the symbols. This is a shortcut. Here are the details of how you must always draw a symbol in order to activate it.

- First you create the shape of the symbol, either tracing its shape, usually with a finger or fingers in the air or over the palm of the other hand, or visualizing it.

- Then tap into the centre of the symbol three times.

- Whilst tapping, recite the symbol's mantra three times.

Draw
The symbols can be drawn any size, from the smallest you can draw, to the biggest you can do with your arm stretched out – big enough to cover your house from a distance. You can draw the symbol with fingers over your recipient or item, with your nose in the air, even on the roof of your mouth with your tongue or by walking the shape of the symbol. Or by tracing the symbol in your mind's eye. In fact the symbol doesn't need to be 'drawn' at all once you are familiar enough with it. It is enough to simply imagine or visualize the symbol where you want it.

Drawing must always be done discreetly if you are with anyone who has not been trained to Reiki II or higher.

You will find that the Distance symbol particularly is quite long. When drawing it you can keep going over the same area, such as the palm of your hand; you don't have to draw it in just one straight line.

Once you have learned the symbols it will rarely be necessary to draw them in ink unless you are teaching them. If you do, literally draw a symbol with pencil or ink, then when you no longer need it you should destroy it by burning, never just put it in the bin.

Tap
The tapping will be done by whatever you have used to draw, so your fingers, tongue, nose, foot or if in your mind's eye, with a slight nodding of the forehead/third eye. Or even just holding the intention to tap it in.

Recite
Reciting the mantra should only be done out loud if you are alone or if everyone present has Reiki II or above. Otherwise it should be said silently in your head. If you are alone the mantra can be said, sung or even chanted.

THE POWER SYMBOL

Also known as the Focus symbol, the Power symbol was not created by Sensei Usui, but derives from Shintoism. A direct translation of the symbol's mantra could be 'direct divine essence', or 'direct mysterious power', or, using Mrs Takata's words 'put the Reiki here'.

The symbol can be viewed as a pictograph, and there are a number of interpretations. Viewed as a whole, the Power symbol can easily be seen as a snake, its body coiled and its head raised, poised to strike; perhaps representative of the coiled snake at the base of the spine, rising up, as spiritual Kundalini energy rises through the chakras to the crown at the moment of enlightenment.

Most commonly, viewed as separate elements, the horizontal line is seen to represent God-consciousness in the heavens. The vertical line then represents a beam of light coming down from the heavens. The spiral is one of the oldest symbols, which has been used in many different cultures from the Neolithic age. Present in nature, for example in a snail shell, DNA or the unfurling of a fern frond, it is easy to see why the spiral has been said to represent Earth and the earthly elements of earth, water, fire and air, which, in this symbol, revolves around space (the void between the lines of the spiral). Alternatively, the spiral can be seen to represent the Self, particularly if you see the vertical line as representative of the hara line, which runs vertically through the centre of our bodies, and note that the spiral intersects

The spiral of the Power symbol lined up with the chakras.

this line seven times, each crossing representing a chakra. So with this symbol we have heavenly light coming down to Earth.

Uses of the Power Symbol

The Power symbol is so called because once you have been attuned to it, you will be able to use this symbol to switch 'Reiki on'. The symbol acts a bit like a combined on/off and volume switch on a radio, so you use the symbol both to switch Reiki on, and to build the intensity. Other than switching Reiki on, it can also be used to protect, to cleanse, to ground and to seal. In healing, the Power symbol is most useful in a physical healing.

Power on/Power up
Draw the symbol on the palm of your hand (and remember, to draw the symbol

first trace it, then tap it three times saying the mantra, silently or in your mind unless you are alone or only with others that have Reiki II. You can draw the symbol on either or both hands. You can also draw the symbol over the person or thing that you are giving Reiki to. You can even draw the symbol on the roof of your mouth to empower your words with Reiki. For manifestation, draw the symbol over a picture or written description of what you are manifesting. Most importantly, the Power symbol can be used to power other symbols.

Protection

Draw the symbol over anyone or anything that you want to protect. You can draw this over yourself, another person or an animal. You can also draw it over your house, your car or any other item that you want to protect. Because Reiki works on every level, using the Power symbol for protection will protect on a physical, emotional, mental and spiritual level. I draw the Power symbol by the side of my bed every morning, so that I step into it and have my protection in place as soon as I get out of bed. You can re-do your protection whenever you feel you need it, and especially if you are somewhere where you need more protection such as in a hospital, shopping centre or a place where you feel vulnerable. Always re-do your protection before giving Reiki.

I once spent the night in a hotel in Scotland. Although I was travelling with work colleagues more senior than me I seemed to have been given the best room in the hotel. It had its own flight of stairs, a huge bathroom, a sitting room with several sofas and a huge four-poster in the bedroom. When it was time for bed I finally understood why I had been given the best room. Going into the room I became aware of a very malicious energetic presence. I was quite frightened! I drew the Power symbol on every side of the bed, over the mattress and over the ceiling – several times. I am glad to say that I slept all night, undisturbed.

Cleansing

Draw the Power symbol over food and drink, supplements and medicines to make sure they are healthy and nourishing and easily digested. *Do not rely on Reiki to make spoiled food or drink edible.*

Grounding

The Power symbol has a low, earthy vibration, and I have used it successfully in grounding myself and others. I often imagine the spiral extending down into the earth under the person or thing I am grounding.

Seal

Draw the symbol over anything that you want to lock in. To seal healing energy in at the end of a healing, especially after performing psychic surgery, draw the symbol over your patient. Or draw the symbol to energetically lock a door, drawer or cupboard that you want to discourage other people from opening.

THE HARMONY SYMBOL

The Harmony symbol is also known as the Balance symbol or the Mental/ Emotional symbol. Helpfully, each name describes its functions. Again the symbol wasn't created by Sensei Usui, and is probably derived from the Sanskrit syllable 'hrih', which has been translated to mean 'meditation and compassion' and is the seed syllable for the Bodhisattva Avalokiteshvara, the 'God who looks down'.[9]

This symbol has a higher vibration than the Power symbol. Direct translations of the Japanese mantra include 'origin', 'original essence', 'one's nature', and also 'idiosyncrasy' and 'habit', and indicate a desire to restore something to its original balance. It is often interpreted as 'as above, so below' or 'God and man coming together'.

The Sanskrit letter 'hrih' – perhaps the derivation of the Harmony symbol.

Uses of the Harmony Symbol

The most obvious use is in healing mental and emotional conditions. It is also very important in physical healing, as many physical complaints are caused by mental or emotional issues.

Aside from healing, the symbol can bring harmony and peace wherever there is conflict. Consider using the symbol to heal any relationships where there is conflict including within families, businesses, between friends, even between animals. Even the internal conflict that causes bad habits or unwanted behaviour such as smoking, drinking or emotional eating can be resolved using the Harmony symbol. Note that when working on relationships it is not always necessary to have the consent of all parties, as Reiki can be sent to the relationship itself, rather than the individuals concerned.

This symbol also increases sensitivity and receptivity, so it can be as powerful in creating new good habits as it is in dispelling old bad ones. It is also very useful in developing new skills and used over the third eye chakra will develop psychic ability.

The symbol is also very effective in removing mental blocks and limiting beliefs.

This symbol always needs to be used together with the Power symbol. Draw the Harmony symbol first and then the Power symbol to power it, or use one symbol in each hand.

Callie and Cleo

Some time ago we decided to get a puppy. Callie was instantly adored by every member of the family – apart from Cleo, our cat. When Callie got too big to be swiped at, poor Cleo retreated upstairs, only ever coming down to dart through the house to her cat flap (often with Callie in playful pursuit!). Sadly it didn't occur to me for quite some time, but eventually I decided to use the Harmony symbol to try to improve their relationship. Little by little Cleo braved coming downstairs, especially at feeding time. Once they were in the same room together it was even easier to put the symbol into the space between them. Callie stopped chasing her, and now they very happily live in the same space.

Callie and Cleo – friends thanks to the Harmony symbol.

THE DISTANCE SYMBOL

The Distance symbol and its mantra are made up of a combination of Japanese kanji. It is often translated as 'having no past, no present and no future', 'a handshake across time and space' or 'the Buddha in me reaches out to the Buddha in you'. This symbol enables you to connect easily and instantly with any person or thing regardless of where they are in both space and time. You might find it hard to believe at first, but I have carried out thousands of distance healings and can promise you that they are extremely effective.

In fact using the Distance symbol seems to make distance healings more powerful and effective than face-to-face healings. Whether this is because the recipient is more comfortable in their own surroundings or whether the symbol itself adds something to the process I am not completely clear, although I understand that Sensei Usui himself preferred to send healing to the patient either across the room or even in the next room.

The Distance symbol is used to provide the connection between the healer and the patient. I usually like to picture the symbol as a bridge leading to the place and time where I am sending Reiki. Once the bridge is in place you can then send Reiki, and either or both of the other symbols, over the bridge to deliver the healing.

Although it is sometimes said that there is no need to use the Distance symbol in a face-to-face healing, in fact I do sometimes use it to connect to the patient on a higher level, or to connect both myself and the patient to Reiki. I even use the Distance symbol to connect myself to my higher self or to Reiki during meditation and self-healing. This is all done by simply holding the appropriate intention while drawing the symbol.

USING SYMBOLS TO PROTECT YOUR HEALING SPACE

It is particularly important to protect any space where you are giving healing, whether or not this is a room that you regularly use for healing, and, once you have Reiki II, whether your recipient is with you in the space or you are sending healing to them elsewhere.

To protect a room, trace a huge Power symbol with your finger in the air in the middle of each wall, ceiling and floor of a room. If you are using a chair or table for the healing, trace the Power symbol over that in the same way. To keep energies in balance, draw the Harmony symbol into each of the corners of the room.

Using Symbols in Healing

You can start to use the symbols as soon as you have been attuned; there is no need to wait until the end of the twenty-one-day clearing period. The symbols will make the Ki stronger, and will enable you to direct Ki more than you can at Reiki I.

To incorporate symbols into healing, first draw the Power symbol in one or both palms to switch 'Reiki on'. Then to use symbols further, you can either draw the symbol on the palm(s) of your hands or draw the symbol over your patient. You can re-draw the symbol when you change hand position, including changing between the symbols. You can use more than one symbol in a hand position either by switching from one symbol to the other, or by placing one symbol in each hand. If you want to stop using a symbol simply brush your hands together a couple of times.

Regarding which symbol to use where, you can use symbols in any of the standard hand positions, or anywhere else where you are giving healing, and you can use any symbol on any chakra. If your client has a closed chakra, or an area of the aura that feels hot, this indicates that stronger healing is needed and you could use the power symbol in that area. If you notice any issues in the mental or emotional area of the aura, use the Harmony symbol. Use your knowledge of the symbols, and your knowledge of your client's condition to indicate which symbol to use where. Of course, if your intuition guides you, have the confidence to follow it. If you do not feel strongly led,

try using the Power symbol for bringing the lower chakras into balance, and the Harmony symbol on the upper chakras.

Just take care if you are giving Reiki to someone who hasn't had it before. Some people are quite sensitive to Ki, and if they haven't experienced it before it might be overwhelming to use the symbols. Most often, for a first healing, I only use the symbols to turn 'Reiki on'. Then I will add symbols to the second and third healings. Always keep at least a soft gaze on your patient, and if they seem to be reacting strongly to the treatment, or are uncomfortable in any way, then stop using symbols until they have become more used to the Ki.

12

ADVANCED HEALING TECHNIQUES

HEALING PAST ISSUES (Reiki II)

Of course it is not possible to change the past. But if we can send Reiki into the past to heal an issue, then we can change the future by changing the impact that the past has on us now.

Past events, whether the harm they caused was physical or emotional, can continue to play a part in our current lives. If we want to move on, it is important to learn the lesson that needs to be learned from these events.

To send healing into a past issue you need to use the Distance symbol to connect to the past event. You can send the healing to an exact date, an approximate date, a place where your client was at the time or to the event itself.

Once you have made the connection you need to switch 'Reiki on', and then you can send the Power and/or the Harmony symbol as appropriate.

Healing a Past Issue with Reiki

Let's say that a client is suffering from a degenerative heart condition. He tells you that he always felt less loved than his brothers. He tells you of a time when, as a child, he received fewer Christmas presents than his siblings.

If you know the year this happened (perhaps the client remembers how old he was at the time) then you can send Reiki to 25 December XXXX. If you don't, you can send to 'the Christmas that John received fewer presents than his brothers'. During the healing,

whenever feels appropriate, draw the Distance symbol and set the intention to send healing to the past event. Send the Harmony symbol to your client in the past. If you have their consent you can also send the Harmony symbol to any parents and siblings. If you don't have consent then you can just send Reiki to the general situation.

Once you feel the flow of Reiki subside, return to the current place and time and complete the healing. You can send healing to the past for as long, and as many times, as seems appropriate.

HEALING WITH THE BREATH AND EYES

Up until now you have learned how to give Reiki through your palm chakras. You might have noticed that you have chakras in your fingertips and in your feet that can send Reiki too. It is also possible to give Reiki through the breath and through the eyes.

These methods are usually incorporated into a healing using the hands as usual, rather than being used as a stand-alone treatment. They can be useful when you want to give Reiki surreptitiously, for example to Reiki your food when you are eating in a restaurant.

Healing with the Breath (Koki-Ho)

Healing with the breath can be quite strong, so don't use this on anyone who isn't experienced in receiving Reiki. For hygiene purposes I only use this technique over the crown of the head or the feet.

To use this method, expand your belly, taking a deep breath imagining that you are drawing Reiki in through the crown of your head all the way down to the tanden. Hold your breath and draw the symbol you want to use onto the roof of your mouth with your tongue. Then breathe the Reiki out, intending that you are breathing Reiki into the area that you are healing.

Healing with the Eyes (Gyoshi-Ho)

To use this method, gaze on the area to be healed. This can be the area you are healing with your hands, or another area. Then allow your eyes to relax out of focus. Form the intention that Reiki flows from your eyes to the area you are gazing at. To add symbols, simply visualize the symbol over the area that you are healing and intend Reiki to flow through it.

THE CIRCLE OF EIGHT (including cord cutting)

This technique can be used to help a client gain closure over an emotional issue, especially where a client needs the opportunity to say goodbye. It can be used to say goodbye to a departed loved one, especially a miscarried or aborted baby, or to get closure from a lover or friend where the parting has been on bad or sad terms. I have also used it with great success in weight-loss and removing limiting beliefs. You can even use it to get rid of a virus or headache, or to put an issue that is worrying you out of your mind.

You can use this technique on its own or as part of a healing.

One of the best things about this technique is that you do not need to know any details of the issue. So you can use this successfully even if your client can't or isn't ready to talk about the issue. You just need to agree how to describe what it is that is being said goodbye to. Most often you can simply use 'the person'; other suggestions could be 'the virus', 'the event', 'the thing', 'the emotion', 'the limiting belief', 'the issue' or 'the fear'. Or you can be more specific. For weight-loss and breaking habits I have used 'sugar', 'fat', 'alcohol' and 'cigarettes'.

Read through the script a few times before you use it so that you are familiar with it. You can change the script as is appropriate and you will need to customize it sufficiently for it to make sense for your client's issue. I usually use this technique with the client sat in a chair opposite me, but you could use it with a client lying down. You might like to offer to make a recording of this part of the healing so that the client can listen to it again over the next few days.

It is possible to use this technique on yourself. To do that, feel free to record the script so you can play it back.

Script

Start by bringing your attention to your breathing. Not necessarily changing the speed or depth of your breathing, just noticing it. Now I'd like you to imagine that you are sitting in your favourite place. It is a beautiful day, the sun is shining and you can hear birds singing.

In your mind's eye, at arm's length draw a circle around yourself. See this circle like a blue neon light around you and know that you are completely safe within its boundaries.

Now create another circle of the same size attached to yours, so that both circles form a figure of eight. Imagine [use the agreed words to describe the person or the issue] *inside the other circle. You may notice that you are connected by strands of energy, or cords, which are attached to different parts of your body. Watch the flow of energy between you. Who takes – who gives?* [Pause here for a moment to allow the client to do this. While you are pausing, draw the Harmony and then the Power symbol into one hand and the Distance and then the Power symbol into the other. Start beaming Reiki to your client whilst reading the next section of the script.]

The Circle of Eight.

Tell [the person/thing] *in the other circle everything that you feel you need to say and everything that you feel they need to hear. Take as much time as you need to do this, and nod your head when you have finished.* [When the client nods you can stop sending Reiki and continue with the next part of the script.]

Now look around you and find a tool on the ground that you can use to cut your energy connections – it could be golden scissors, bolt cutters, whatever seems right to you. Pick them up and cut the cords. If you can, state in your mind that you forgive [the person/thing] *for any upset that they have caused you.*

[Draw the Power symbol into the palm of one hand and start to beam Reiki while you read the next part of the script.] *Take some time now to thank* [the person/thing] *for the lesson that you have learned through them, and nod when you have finished.* [Keep sending Reiki until the client nods, then stop sending Reiki and continue with the last part of the script.] *Now see the blue light around you increase in intensity and see the other circle detach. Watch the circle float away with* [the person/thing] *happy and smiling/harmless/released* [choose the appropriate term]. *Nod when you have finished.* [Pause] *Acknowledge that you are both free now and when you are ready, open your eyes.*

Give your patient a glass of water to make sure they are grounded. Talk about their experience as much as is appropriate.

ADVANCED MENTAL/EMOTIONAL HEALING

This very powerful technique can be used alone or at the start of a standard treatment when the issue you are dealing with has a mental or emotional cause. If you are using the technique as part of a full healing you will be able to reduce the time spent on the other hand positions, so for an hour's healing you could use this technique for thirty minutes, then use the standard hand positions (or follow your intuition) for the remaining time. There is a lot to remember here, but feel free to just use parts of the technique while you familiarize yourself with it, to write bullet points on a card which you can glance at during the healing, and don't feel that you need to follow every part of this to the letter.

As we are working with the Harmony symbol and in the crown chakra it is critical to keep positive thoughts in your mind, to focus solely on your client, and not to let yourself be distracted. It is therefore important to spend more time than usual on your preparation. The client will usually be lying down, and you need to be seated to the side of the client's head on the side where the hand that you write with is at the head end, the other hand towards the foot end.

1. Make sure that you are grounded, your aura is clear and that you have your protection in place. Draw the Power symbol into one or both hands, and give yourself Reiki for a

few moments (follow your intuition, but I suggest either at the heart or third eye, or one hand on each).

2. Set a positive intention, for example that this healing be to the recipient's highest good. Place the foot-end hand under the back of the recipient's head. With the other hand, you are going to draw symbols in the crown chakra, intending that they travel in through the crown, then through each chakra to the heart. First draw the Distance symbol, intending it to connect you and your client to Reiki, then the Harmony symbol for mental/emotional healing and then the Power symbol. Finally place your hand on the crown of the head.

3. Imagine soft white light flowing from the palm of your hand in through the crown to fill the recipient's head. As you continue to send Reiki, visualize it flowing slowly and gradually through the recipient's body. (You can spend several minutes doing this.) Once you have filled the body with soft white light, starting again at the crown, send a rainbow of coloured light first to fill the head and then the whole body. Then repeat again, this time with bright white light. Once the body is filled with this bright white light imagine it spilling out from the body into the aura, and then filling the whole room.

4. Keeping the hands one behind the head and the other on the crown,

imagine a strand of bright white light coming from the recipient's heart and solar plexus, joining and spiralling upwards. Imagine it spiralling up all the way out of the room, up into the sky and up to the edge of the Earth's atmosphere. Continue the spiral up above the atmosphere and into space, travelling past planets and stars towards the centre of the Universe. As you travel towards the centre of the Universe imagine that you can start to see the Source, the creator of all. This is the source of all the love and light that has ever been and will ever be. Visualize it as golden light. Continue to move closer to the Source, and when you reach it, connect the spiral strands to it. Then start to notice this Source light travelling down the spiral strands bringing love and light and joy. See this light filling your patient, travelling through every fibre to every cell of the body, bringing healing at the deepest level. When you feel this process is completed, imagine disconnecting the strands from the Source at the centre of the Universe, and bring the ends all the way back to the patient. Take the hand from the crown and seal the ends back into the heart and solar plexus by drawing the Power symbol over each of them, and then draw the Power symbol over the crown to seal there using an appropriate affirmation, such as 'I seal in this healing with love and light.'

5. If you are continuing on to a full healing, you can just join your hands at the back of the head and continue the healing from there. If you are finishing, move to the feet and ground the recipient before smoothing the aura and gently waking them as usual.

PSYCHIC SURGERY

The word 'surgery' usually means cutting a patient open and removing or repairing tissue. Psychic surgery means the removal, not of tissue, but of energy, energy blocks and other things at an energetic level that are present in the body or aura of the client which are not healthy. Thankfully with psychic surgery there is no actual cutting!!

Although a general Reiki healing will remove and repair these things, it doesn't do it very quickly, and several healings may be needed before blocks are removed sufficiently to even let Reiki in. It can be helpful to perform psychic surgery to remove the item quickly and easily so that Reiki can immediately flow in and start the healing process.

To perform psychic surgery you can use your hand, a wand or a crystal point. Use the point of the wand or crystal to direct a beam of energy, which can penetrate into the body if required, to 'cut' around the edge of what you are removing. Then either hold the crystal over the area, allowing it to absorb everything that you want removed, or using an upward spiralling motion use the wand to draw out the energy you are removing. Flick the wand or crystal in the direction of the floor to clear out the energy that has accumulated, and continue until you have removed all that you need to.

If you are using your hand, first protect each of the finger chakras by drawing a Power symbol over each fingertip, then just use your fingers to scoop out the negative energy or energy blocks. If what you are removing is in the physical body rather than the aura, intend that your aura will form extensions to your fingers that can penetrate the skin so that you can reach into the body to remove what you need to. Drop the removed energy to the floor with the intention that it be neutralized.

When you are finished be sure to cleanse yourself and the crystal and/or wand thoroughly. Hold the intention that all the energy that was removed has been neutralized.

Once you have removed all that you need to, line the 'wound' that is left by smoothing it over and applying first the Harmony and then the Power symbol. Most importantly, fill the space left with Reiki. When the repair is complete, seal it by drawing the Power symbol over it.

13

BECOMING A REIKI PRACTITIONER

It is a wonderful thing to choose to dedicate your time and energy to healing others, and it will bring great rewards. I often receive cards and messages from clients and students thanking me and telling me how Reiki has changed their lives – I never got that in twenty-five years of working as a lawyer!! It is possible to make a good living as a healer. However you will find that if making money is your primary motivation you are much less likely to succeed. Many more people are discovering the benefits of Reiki, and people in general are starting to take more responsibility for their health instead of expecting their GP to have a pill to cure all ills. As more people turn to Reiki, more good practitioners are needed.

References in this book to legal and regulatory requirements refer only to those requirements in the UK. Requirements in other jurisdictions will be different. Please research these elsewhere.

REGULATORY REQUIREMENTS

In the UK we are extremely fortunate to have a regulatory system that maintains a balance between giving practitioners the freedom to practice many of the varied styles of Reiki and yet still offers protection to members of the public. Although the US government body tasked with studying the safety and efficacy of complementary and integrative health practice, the National Center for Complementary and Integrative Health, states on their website[10] that 'Reiki hasn't been shown to have any harmful effects', nevertheless a number of US states are currently seeking to impose a licensing system on the practice of complementary therapies including Reiki. Whilst on the face of it licensing could be seen as a good thing, the fact that the cost of a license could be as much as $8,000 will force many complementary practitioners to give up their practice.

There are in fact no regulatory requirements for the practice of Reiki in the UK. There are two regulatory bodies that operate to regulate the activities of Reiki practitioners that choose to register with them, but registration is optional.

Although there are no restrictions concerning your ability to work as a Reiki practitioner in the UK, this does not mean that you should not take an extremely professional approach to your development as a Reiki practitioner. In fact, requirements much stronger than regulation should govern your practice. Primarily, your practice needs to be motivated by love, and by a desire to help your clients. You need to follow as closely as possible the Reiki Principles. You need to keep a faithful daily practice of self-healing. Overall, it is important to Reiki, the reputation of holistic therapy and to yourself to always act professionally and with the utmost integrity.

QUALIFICATION REQUIREMENTS

Although I don't know where the practice began, it seems to be widely accepted now that in order to work as a practitioner you need at least Reiki II. We know it isn't due to the ability to channel Reiki, as Mrs Takata worked in Hayashi's clinic as a healer for a year before she was awarded her level II. However, employers and insurers seem to consider a Reiki II certificate to be an indication that you have the pre-requisites to work as a practitioner.

In truth, the skills that you learn at Reiki II will be extremely helpful to you in working as a practitioner. And because it has become practice, most Reiki Master Teachers include content in their Reiki II classes that is geared towards working as a practitioner. So for the purposes of this chapter I have assumed that you have attained Reiki II before working as a practitioner.

Verified Reiki Practitioners

In the UK at present, registration of Reiki Practitioners is voluntary, and most choose not to register. However if you would like to register you can choose to register either with The Reiki Council or with the Complementary & Natural Healthcare Council (CNHC). Registration with The Reiki Council will automatically include registration with either the CNHC or the General Regulatory Council for Complementary Therapies (GRCCT). The route to verification is not actually through The Reiki Council itself, but through one of its approved member organizations.

Approved Member Organizations

- The Reiki Alliance
- The Reiki Association
- The Reiki Connection
- The Reiki Guild
- UK Reiki Federation
- Complementary and Natural Healthcare Council

Because Reiki is taught and practised in many different ways, and The Reiki Council has an objective to uphold the freedom to practice the different styles, there are no fixed criteria for verification. You will be able to work through the requirements with your chosen member organization, but as a guide you will probably need:

- To have carried out perhaps as many as seventy-five full treatments (including distance treatments), a number of which have been supervised.

- To have practised Reiki for at least nine months since you took your Reiki I and perhaps even as long as two years.

- Detailed case studies, or client reviews.

- A number of hours both face-to-face and distance learning that will certainly exceed your Reiki I and II courses, and may include Reiki Shares.

- To practise in accordance with the National Occupational Standards.

- Evidence of continual professional development.

(You should also be aware that although The Reiki Council are careful to be inclusive of the many different Reiki styles, they will not accept online attunements or Holy Fire ignitions as sufficient, and face-to-face attunements at each level are required.)

It is clear from these extensive requirements for registration that you will not be eligible to register as you start out as a beginner. However, simple membership of one of the approved member organizations or other complementary therapy organizations will often satisfy a potential employer's requirements.

PROFESSIONALISM

Professional Standards (UK)

In the UK there are three National Occupational Standards (NOS) that apply to the professional practice of Reiki (only one is specific to Reiki). Details of the requirements of these standards can be found through skillsforhealth.org.uk. NOS do not have legal effect, but are designed to 'ensure... the UK has a competent, flexible and safe workforce which can drive the growth of a productive, globally competitive and sustainable economy.'[11]

Complementary & Natural Healthcare (CNH) 1 – *therapist must have the ability to explore and establish the client's needs and expectations.*

- Exploring and establishing the client's needs and expectations is an ongoing process that will start with your first communication, and will continue as long as you have a professional relationship with the client. You will obtain valid and reliable information concerning the needs of your client through observation, conversation and use of your intuition. Make sure that you encourage your client to ask questions and express any concerns, so that this is truly a two-way process.

■ You must have a safe and appropriate space in which to practice Reiki, where the client can feel welcomed and comfortable. (This can include using your client's premises.)

■ You are required to keep appropriate records.

Complementary & Natural Healthcare (CNH) 2 – *therapist must have the ability to discuss and agree a care plan with the client.*

■ Use the information gained to discuss and agree a healing plan with your client. Ensure that your client understands your fee structure. Reiki is beneficial in all situations, but with some conditions, other referrals (perhaps to your client's doctor) or healing methods might be appropriate, and if this is the case you must inform your client.

■ As a holistic therapy, Reiki treats the whole person, not just their symptoms. Accordingly, most clients will need a good number of treatments for them to be completely healed, and both you and your client will need to be patient. You need to be sure to set your client's expectations as to how many treatments might be necessary. For reasons discussed in earlier chapters it is a good idea for every course of treatments to begin with at least three in fairly quick succession.

Complementary & Natural Healthcare (CNH) 12 – *therapist must have the ability to use Reiki non-invasively and holistically to restore balance in body, mind and spirit, and must keep up to date.*

■ The requirements of this standard are very comprehensive. Rather than repeat them here, I can assure you that provided you take a reputable Reiki I and II class and read this book you will have covered it!

Ethics

Doctors of Western medicine in many countries take some form of oath, many of which are based on the Hippocratic Oath, said to have been written by Hippocrates who lived between 460–570 BCE. Several parts of the Hippocratic Oath are perhaps not relevant today, but several parts of it are as relevant today as they were when they were written over 2,000 years ago.

'I will keep (the sick) from harm and injustice.'

Often translated as 'first, do no harm'. Taken literally, with Western medicine it is almost impossible to comply with this part of the oath. Needles and scalpels cut and bruise. So it is interpreted as a balance of risk; it is acceptable to do harm if the possible benefits outweigh the risks. Surely this too is in many cases impossible to forecast. What must be required is at least the recognition that whilst physicians can do great good, they can also do harm.[12]

Reiki itself can do no harm. Strive that you too do no harm.

'In purity and holiness I will guard my life and my art.'

Confidentiality

'What I may see or hear in the course of treatment or even outside of the treatment in regard to the life of men, which on no account one must spread abroad, I will keep to myself, holding such things shameful to be spoken about.'

Hippocratic Oath, translation

When you work as a Reiki practitioner it is essential to keep up with your self-healing practice. It is by taking care of yourself that you are in the best position to take care of your clients. Make sure you use Reiki on your business too.

There is no oath taken by Reiki practitioners. But you need to commit to behave ethically in your Reiki practice. How you do this is up to you. You might just leave it to be implied. Or you could choose a Code of Ethics that you agree to adhere to. You could include the code on your website. Most Reiki organizations have a code of ethics they expect their members to adhere to, and members can refer to this code on their website.

Reiki as a Holistic Complementary Therapy

Reiki is a complementary therapy, meaning that it complements other therapies. Because it is a holistic therapy Reiki can be used to heal every illness or condition, whether chronic or acute and whether its symptoms or cause are physical, mental or emotional. However, Reiki is not always the quickest or most suitable therapy for every condition, and it is your duty as a Reiki practitioner to recommend other healing modalities to your client if you believe they would be more suitable. For example, a client with a bad back might obtain relief more quickly from seeing a chiropractor or osteopath. A client with a broken bone obviously needs it re-set in hospital. Reiki can then be used alongside this other form of healing to speed up healing and relieve pain, and this complementary use of Reiki is recommended for anyone being treated allopathically with Western medicine.

COMMUNICATION

Aside from being able to give a lovely, relaxing Reiki treatment, the most important skill you need in order to be a successful Reiki practitioner is to be a good communicator. Good communication skills can make the client feel at ease, create trust, set the client's expectations and help understanding of the needs of your client. Plus, enabling your client to feel that they have been really heard and understood by being a good listener is an important part of the healing process. If you are open to taking additional training, I highly recommend you taking a communication skills class.

Other than making the appointment, taking client details and a brief medical history will probably be the first conversation with your client. A template client information form is set out in Appendix B but do check with your insurer's particular requirements as they are all different. Rather than regarding this step as paperwork to get out of the way, use the time to help your client settle in. I usually give the client the form to complete their details and then sign the consent, but then take the form back and get the client to talk through their medical history. Many people are never happier than when they are talking about their ailments, so this will start to build a rapport between you, and you will not only learn about the issue they have come to you about but perhaps also the underlying cause(s).

Language

It is important in communicating with the client to always be positive and supportive. We already know that energetically like attracts like, so if your client comes to you full of despair and without hope, it is important that you lift their mood not only with Reiki, but also in the way that you communicate. That you are taking time to bring them healing can make them feel worthy of love, and take away feelings of helplessness. Lifting the mood in this way raises the energetic vibration and helps the body to heal.

Make sure you use language that your client understands, so perhaps don't talk to them about a 'blocked heart chakra' unless you know that they understand what this means. Instead you might say that you found an energy block that Reiki will clear.

It is very important that you *never* give a diagnosis. Sometimes a client will come to you thinking that you are psychic, and will refuse to tell you the issue they want healed! Actually, the more you do Reiki the more psychic you will become, and sometimes you will pick up information either from the client's aura or chakras, or just an impression you get during the healing. Try to discern whether it is appropriate for you to communicate the information to your client, and if you do, be very sensitive about how you do so.

All the time that you are talking with your client it is important to watch their body language. Notice whether they seem relaxed or ill at ease. Often clients will not be completely honest when they are talking to you. This might be because they are embarrassed about their lifestyle choices and don't want to feel judged, or because they are not comfortable talking about the issue that they have. Perhaps they are not even being honest with themselves. Ironically, it isn't important from a Reiki point of view whether the client is being honest or not, as Reiki is always going to go where it needs to go and work to the client's highest good, even if neither you nor the client know what that is! Try using the Circle of Eight technique detailed in Chapter 12, Advanced Healing Techniques, for a condition that the client is really unable to talk to you about.

SETTING UP YOUR BUSINESS

Legal Considerations

Unless you choose to set up a limited company then you will be regarded as a sole trader. As a sole trader you are legally responsible for everything that you do in your business. There is no legal requirement to have a separate business bank account, but you will need to check that your bank allows your personal bank account to be used by a business. You need to keep a separate record of all money moving in and out of the business. You don't need to register for VAT until your business income reaches the VAT threshold, which at the time of writing is £85,000.

The main advantage of setting up a limited company is that you are not automatically responsible for any damage caused by your business (in other words, your liability is limited). The reason is that your business has its own identity. Other consequences of this are that it must have a separate bank account, and that any income belongs to the company, not to you. There are usually extra costs in running a limited company, such as bank charges and audit fees.

However you structure your business you should have some simple contract terms and conditions. You may be able to obtain some standard terms through a complementary therapy association. If you want to write your own, think about what is most important to your business and explain these rules in clear and simple language, for example payment terms, cancellation charges and so on.

Insurance

You must be insured. It is very unlikely that anyone will ever make a claim that Reiki has done any harm. But if a client falls off your treatment table, or trips over your doormat, they may be able to claim compensation. I recommend public liability and professional indemnity insurance of at least £1 million each. You may also want to add contents insurance. If you have any employees, you must by law have employers' liability insurance. Some complementary organizations offer discounts on insurance to members.

Financial Records

You must keep a separate record of all business-related financial transactions, both what you pay out and what you receive. These records need to be used to complete your tax return each year. You will need to choose whether to use a simple spreadsheet, an online app, or an accountant or bookkeeper.

Tax

If you are employed (even by your *own* limited company) you will be taxed via PAYE (Pay As You Earn), which means that tax will be deducted before you receive your salary.

If you are a sole trader you are self-employed and you must complete a tax return every year. You will get a tax bill at the end of the year, so make sure you keep enough income saved to pay it. Any business expenses are tax deductible, that is you deduct the costs from your income before your tax is assessed.

Things you can claim against taxes include: all your materials and capital purchases for your clinic (for example, the items on the equipment list), cost of rent, advertising, telephone charges, hosting charges, staff salaries, a percentage of motoring costs and phone costs, professional memberships and subscriptions, clothing, business dining, even the magazines you buy for your waiting room. But you must keep all receipts.

You must pay National Insurance contributions and should pay into a private pension under the stakeholder pension scheme.

CHARGING

The best way to work out what you should charge for giving Reiki is to look at other businesses in your area offering Reiki or similar services such as sports massage, reflexology, acupuncture or even coaching or counselling, then use their pricing as a guide. Work out the range of prices for similar services and then carry out an honest assessment of your offering. Reiki can be offered for as little as £35 per hour where someone uses a spare room in their house to as much as £120 per hour in a beautiful spa.

Although the second Reiki precept is that you obtain an exchange of value for giving Reiki, it is acceptable for you to offer highly discounted or even free Reiki when you are trying to establish your practice. When I started, I offered seven free treatments followed by seven half-price treatments, which brought me seven new clients very rapidly, and seven more quite quickly after that. Those clients will then recommend you to their family and friends.

Use pricing tactics to make sure your client gets the full benefit of Reiki by coming back for at least three treatments. Offer a special price for buying a course of three treatments, or maybe even three treatments for the price of two.

CREATING A BUSINESS PLAN

It might seem quite daunting, and too business-like, to think of creating a business plan. You might think that it is unnecessary if you are not going to be setting up a business bank account or borrowing money. But it is very useful to go though the process of narrowing down the detail of what you are going to do, and putting it into writing. Also once you have the plan, you can use it as a basis for manifestation.

What

Describe what you are going to sell. Your business could be selling services (healing, teaching, coaching) or products (tangible or intangible, such as downloads), or both.

Is Reiki central to your business, or are you adding Reiki to something else that you already do? To work with Reiki you don't need to completely change what you already do (although of course you can if you want to!). I have students who are very successfully incorporating Reiki into their businesses, for example one is a very popular window cleaner, who Reikis the water he uses!

You

Take some time to examine your motivations. If you are concerned that your motivations are more around making money than they are around helping others, take some time to dig a little deeper. Remember that you are entitled to make a living from helping people, but also there are many easier ways of making money!

Write down your qualifications, experience and all the training that you have done. Review the list and allow it to give you confidence in your abilities. Add a section on your skills, hobbies and interests, and while you do this think of how you can incorporate any of these into your business. Finally, add any training that you need.

Who

Describe here your typical customer: age, gender, location, size of business, business sector. Are your customers individuals or businesses, or both?

Essentially this is market research, but don't be put off by that phrase. Market research is simply understanding your customer. Understanding your customer

is key to creating an atmosphere in which they feel comfortable, whether that is the look and feel of your website, the tone of your social media site, your location, decor and so on.

How

Probably the biggest question here is whether you want to work by yourself or with/for others. There are more opportunities than you might think for working in hospices, nursing homes or hospitals for example. They may have specific qualification requirements, and/or require you to join a professional association. These might impact your 'when', but they shouldn't impact your 'what'.

Equipment

You will need to think about, and cost out, the equipment that you will need. Keep a list of all that you buy and the receipts (a digital photo is sufficient), as these are business expenses that are tax deductible.

It is not necessary to buy everything new. Some suppliers offer discounts for trade buyers if you register in advance.

If you are setting up as a Reiki therapist you will likely need:

- Treatment couch or chair, couch-roll and washable covers.

- Blanket, pillow and cushion for under the knees (lying on back) or ankles (lying on front).

- Music player and music (legally you need a music license to play most music in public).

- Smudge sticks, incense, candles, essential oils, dowsing pendulum, crystals.

- Computer and phone.

- Decoration for your room.

Where

Working from home, perhaps converting a room in your house or using a garden room, saves money and commuting time. If you are having clients visit you at home, make sure to think about:

- How you would cope with an emergency;

  - Take first-aid training.

  - For clients with conditions that you are not trained to manage, for example epilepsy, ask them to bring a carer or family member with them.

- Your personal safety.

Alternatively you can rent a room in a clinic, health centre, spa or sports centre. It can look more professional, and the building itself might bring in clients.

The other alternative is to go mobile, giving treatments at the client's house or business premises.

Above all, try and put yourself into your client's shoes and sort out anything that might cause anxiety. Make sure clients can find you and park easily, there is somewhere for them to leave their coat and bag, you have somewhere comfortable to sit and talk before and after the treatment. Remember that the greatest value of a Reiki healing is the level of relaxation achieved. The more relaxed your client is, the better the healing they will receive.

When

Consider whether you are ready to start straight away, or whether you need time to take more training or build up some stock. Also, whether you can start full time or if you need to start part time, and add more hours as the business grows.

Summary

Once you have written all the above, go back to the beginning and create a summary page, setting out the items that are the most key to your idea.

On this summary page add a business name. Your business is something aside from you. It is important to give it an identity as soon as you can.

Use this summary in manifesting a successful business (*see* 'Using Reiki in Manifestation' in Chapter 10).

RELEVANT LAW

There are no laws that specifically refer to Reiki, or, in the UK, to hands-on healing. But there are a number of laws that could be relevant to your Reiki practice. This is just an outline, and if you are at all uncertain you should take your own legal advice.

S4(1) Cancer Act 1939

It is illegal to advertise an offer to treat, a remedy for, or advice regarding the treatment of cancer. Please note that this restriction only relates to *advertising*, it does not restrict you from treating clients with cancer.

Advertising Standards

Ensure that other advertising is not misleading or offensive in any way.

Notifiable Diseases

There are a number of diseases that are notifiable by law if diagnosed by a registered medical practitioner (that is, registered by the General Medical Council.[13] So unless you are also a registered medical practitioner this law does not apply to you in your capacity of a Reiki practitioner. Also, as a Reiki practitioner you are not qualified to diagnose diseases, and you would likely not recognize the disease if a client did have it. If you are at all concerned, the list is available from the Government website (www.gov.uk, search 'Notifiable Diseases') and there is never any harm in advising a client to talk to their GP, as long as you do it sensitively.

s19 Veterinary Surgeons Act 1966

It is illegal to give people the impression that you are a qualified vet unless you are one. Unless you are a vet it is illegal to diagnose animals and give advice in accordance with that diagnosis.

When working with animals I ask the caregiver to see a vet first to secure the diagnosis.

Suicide Act 1961

It is an offence to encourage or assist anyone to commit suicide. Thankfully when giving Reiki we are rarely put into a spot where either we are working with someone so disturbed that they may be considering suicide or so ill that they are considering euthanasia. Just be aware that contrary to some popular thinking there is no general duty to report suicidal thoughts, and to do so may be in breach of your client's right to confidentiality.

Health & Safety at Work Act 1974

As long as you don't have employees then your obligations under health & safety legislation are minimal. It will be sufficient for you to spend some time assessing the risks to any clients or other members of the public that might come to your property, doing what you can to lessen these risks and keeping a first-aid kit. Obvious things to consider might be any loose rugs that someone may trip over, a treatment table that is adjustable and perhaps a step to help a shorter client climb up and down.

Data Protection Act 2018 and GDPR

To comply with NOS and your insurer, you should keep client records. These records should include at least the client's personal contact details, a medical history, and a record of the treatment given which should include details of any unusual reactions to the treatment. (A template client record is set out in Appendix B.)

To comply with data protection laws the form must contain a signed consent, and this will also operate as your consent to the treatment under the Reiki precepts.

Records must be kept confidential and so it is important that they are kept securely. You can choose to keep physical records, in which case you must ensure they are filed accurately in a locked cabinet; or to keep records on a computer, in which case the computer must have password protection. Records should not be kept on a mobile device (for example a memory stick) unless they are encrypted.

Advice on how long you should keep these records varies. The GRCCT advises six years from the date of last treatment, The Reiki Council advises seven years, and the CNHC advises eight years from the date of last treatment. GDPR requires that data is kept only so long as it is needed. On this basis, I have to say that I think these storage periods are in general far too long. Whilst core financial records are needed for seven years, as the tax authorities have power to investigate back that far, and contractual documents should be kept for six years as contractual claims can be made for six years afterwards, I am not clear as to why client records, unless they are in any way unusual, should be kept for anything like these periods. Most data

breaches happen by accident. Therefore the less data you hold the less chance there is of making a mistake. So my recommendation is to keep each record for as short a time as possible, maybe only six months to one year from the end of treatment. Ultimately, you will need to keep the records for as long as your insurer, or any other organizations of which you are a member, requires.

Music Licence

Most music that you are likely to play during treatments is subject to copyright, including streamed music and YouTube, and you will need to obtain a licence from PPL PRS Ltd (a combination of the Performing Right Society and Phonographic Performance Limited). A small premises licence should be all that you need and at the time of writing costs less than £100 per year. If you don't want to buy a licence, ensure you only play royalty-free music.

Depending upon your circumstances, other legislation such as The Companies Act and The Employment Act may apply to you, but these are beyond the scope of this book.

DEVELOPING YOUR OWN STYLE

At Reiki I you learn how to carry out a healing using a set of standard hand positions. At Reiki II you learn how to use symbols to enhance your healing. The more you use Reiki, the more intuitive you will become about which hand

positions and symbols to use. You will probably soon find that no two healings are the same.

Now is the time to think about developing your own Reiki style. This might start with how you furnish your

Reiki space or treatment room. Consider whether you will use Reiki on its own or combine it with other complementary therapies.

Try to pick up ideas from other life experiences, such as hotels or spas that you have visited, and treatments you have had. Consider whether you have other skills and interests that you can incorporate into your Reiki practice and treatments, such as crystal healing, sound healing, Oracle cards, NLP or tapping.

Above all, use Reiki in as many aspects of your life as you can. The only limits here are the limits you place on yourself and on Reiki. Ask Reiki to help you remove those limits, and consult Reiki on all your important decisions. Even ask Reiki to help you find more opportunities for using Reiki! If you let Reiki into your life in this way, your life will be transformed. You will have a life more wonderful than you could ever have imagined.

May the blessing of Reiki be with you, now and always.

ENDNOTES

1   Chuang-Tzu, *The True Book of the Southern Land of Blossoms* (400BCE)

2   'Staying Healthy – Understanding the stress response' (Harvard Health Publishing, July 6, 2020)

3   Byrne, Rhonda, *The Secret* (Simon & Schuster UK, 2006)

4   Arjava Petter, Frank, *Reiki – The Legacy of Dr Usui* (Lotus Press, 1998)

5   From the inscription on the Usui Memorial, Saihoji Temple, Tokyo

6   Michio Kaku, Theoretical Physicist

7   Translation from etymonline.com

8   Mackenzie Clay, A. J., *The Challenge to Teach Reiki* (New Dimensions, 1992)

9   www.visiblemantra.org

10 National Center for Complementary and Integrative Health, www.nccih.nih.gov/ [accessed April 12, 2021]

11 NOS Strategy 2010–2020 v.2, June 2011

12 Shmerling, Robert H. MD, Harvard Health Blog, 'First, do no harm', (Harvard Health Publishing, June 22, 2020)

13 Health Protection (Notification) Regulations 2010.

APPENDICES

APPENDIX A: MAJOR CHAKRAS AND THEIR FUNCTIONS AND ASSOCIATIONS

Name	Location	Body	Gland	Mental/ emotion	Malfunction	Colour	Note/ sound	Age	Crystal
7. Crown	Top of head	Upper brain, right eye	Pituitary	Boundlessness, understanding	Depression, boredom, confusion, apathy, Alzheimer's, epilepsy	Violet or white	B Om	43–49, 92–98	Amethyst, diamond, clear quartz, selenite
6. Third eye	Between eyes	Lower brain, left eye, ears, nose, nervous system	Pineal	Visualization, psychic ability, intuition, wisdom	Poor vision, headaches, insomnia, nightmares, amnesia, hallucinations	Indigo	A Ah	36–42, 85–91	Lapis lazuli, quartz, Iolite, sodalite, kyanite
5. Throat	Neck	Neck, vocal cords, alimentary canal, teeth, jaw, shoulders	Thyroid Parathyroid	Communication, expression, speak your truth, creativity	Sore throat, stiff neck, colds, thyroid problems, hearing problems	Blue	G Ha	29–35, 78–84	Turquoise, blue lace agate, aquamarine, blue calcite, celestite
4. Heart	Heart	Heart, lungs, blood, circulatory, arms, hands	Thymus	Universal love, empathy, compassion	High blood pressure, heart disease, lung disease, loneliness	Green	F Ya-mm	22–28, 71–77	Emerald, tourmaline, rose quartz
3. Solar plexus	Centre, below ribs	Stomach, liver, gall bladder, nervous system, muscles	Pancreas	Willpower, self-confidence, career	Ulcers, diabetes, hypoglycaemia, fatigue, anxiety, self-doubt	Yellow	E Ra	15–21, 64–70	Amber, topaz, sunstone

(Continued)

Continued

Name	Location	Body	Gland	Mental/ emotion	Malfunction	Colour	Note/ sound	Age	Crystal
2. Sacral	Abdomen	Reproductive system, kidney, bladder	Gonads	Pleasure, *joie de vivre*, desire, sexuality, libido	Impotence, frigidity, UTI, stiff lower back, apathy	Orange	D Ba	8–14, 57–63	Coral, tiger's eye, carnelian, moonstone
1. Root	Base of spine	Spine, bones, kidneys, large intestine, legs, feet	Adrenals	Vitality, grounding, survival, food, shelter	Haemorrhoids, constipation, arthritis, knee trouble	Red	C La	1–7, 50–56	Ruby, bloodstone, garnet

APPENDIX B

Client Information Form (Human)

Name:	Gender:	DOB:
Address:		
		Postcode:
Contact number:		Email:
Next of kin contact details:		
GP name and address:		
		Tel:
Have you had Reiki before? Yes/No If so, was it a pleasant experience? Yes/No		
If no, please describe why not:		
How did you hear about me?		

Consent

I understand that Reiki is a simple, gentle, hands-on energy technique that brings the body into balance and allows it to relax enabling and boosting the body's own healing process. I understand that Reiki practitioners do not diagnose conditions, nor do they prescribe medical treatment or medication, nor will Reiki interfere with any treatment or medication prescribed by my doctor. I understand that Reiki complements, but doesn't take the place of, any medical or psychological treatments that I might be receiving.

I acknowledge that Reiki works holistically to bring health and well-being and that long term imbalances in the body require multiple sessions in order to heal.

I understand that my details will be retained by the practitioner but will not be shared with any third party without prior consent.

Signed _____   Date _____

Medical History

Asthma:	Yes/No	
Back pain:	Yes/No	
Diabetes:	Yes/No	
Epilepsy:	Yes/No	
Heart condition:	Yes/No	
Hypertension:	Yes/No	
Headaches:	Yes/No	
Mental issues:	Yes/No	
Addictions:	Yes/No	
Operations:	Yes/No	
Injuries:	Yes/No	
Allergies:	Yes/No	
Sensitive to touch:	Yes/No	
SAD:	Yes/No	
Current medications:		

Reiki Therapy Form

Client name:	Date:

Reason for visit:

Changes since last visit:

Client mood:

Aura scan:

Chakra (for example open, partially open, closed, clockwise/anti-clockwise):

Base:

Sacral:

Solar plexus:

Heart:

Throat:

Brow:

Crown:

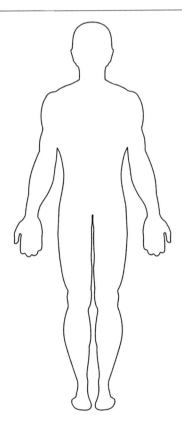

Treatment notes:

Psychic awareness:

Client feedback:

Follow-up visit recommended: Yes/No   Next visit date:

Client Information Form (Animal)

Caregiver's name:		Date:	
Address:		Tel:	

Pet's name:		Age:	
Vet:		Tel:	

I understand that Reiki is a non-medical, non-surgical therapy that complements and supports other healing therapies, but is not a substitute for professional veterinary treatment.

I confirm that I have consulted a vet about any existing medical conditions of which I am aware.

Signed: _____

	Reason for visit
Condition:	
Date of diagnosis:	
Treatment to date:	
Areas identified by Reiki scan	

Comments:

First Visit – Continued

	Chakras – areas of blockage
Crown:	
Third eye:	
Throat:	
Heart:	
Solar plexus:	
Sacral:	
Root:	

	Conclusion
Response to Reiki treatment:	
Further treatment required:	

Follow-up visit
No

Caregiver's name:		Pet's name:	

Follow-up:		Date:	
Results since previous treatment:			
Current condition:			

	Chakras – areas of blockage	Changes noted
Crown:		
Third eye:		
Throat:		
Heart:		
Solar plexus:		
Sacral:		
Root:		

APPENDIX C: TREATMENT CHECKLIST

Before Treatment:

- Prepare the room
  - Clean and tidy
  - Energetically clear
  - Treatment table or chair prepared
  - Candles/music/incense
  - Glass of water available (if face-to-face treatment)
- Prepare yourself
  - Silence phone (once client has arrived)
  - Sweep your aura, ground yourself and put your protection in place
  - Clean and tidy
  - No jewellery
  - Centred
- Prepare the client
  - Client information form (for a paid-for treatment)
  - Remove jewellery/belt
  - Describe treatment
  - Glass of water available (if distance treatment)

During Treatment

- Sweep your aura, ground and protect yourself.

- Invite in Reiki guides to assist, and set intention for the healing.
- Check chakras with pendulum.
- 'Reiki On'/Power symbol.
- Give treatment.
- Scan aura (I usually do this after I have done the hand positions on the head).
- Ground client (always end a treatment on the feet, securing the grounding).
- Smooth aura.
- Re-test chakras.
- Make brief notes of treatment (if a paid-for treatment).
- Wake client.

After Treatment

- Glass of water.
- Discuss treatment.
- Discuss medication (no changes should be made to medication without GP advice).
- Book next treatment.
- Complete client notes (if a paid-for treatment).

APPENDIX D: CASE STUDY

(Suggested format)

Your name and address:

Client ID (not their real name for confidentiality reasons):

Visit 1

Preparation

Preparing the room:

Preparing myself:

Preparing the client:

Treatment (include testing chakras, aura scan, intention, symbols used, client reactions and so on):

After treatment (include client feedback, advice given, follow up appointments discussed and so on):

Visit 2 (feel free to use 'ditto' where you do the same as day 1, and so on)

Preparation

Preparing the room:

Preparing myself:

Preparing the client:

Treatment (include testing chakras, aura scan, intention, symbols used, client reactions and so on):

After treatment (include client feedback, advice given, follow up appointments discussed, etc.):

Visit 3

Preparation

Preparing the room:

Preparing myself:

Preparing the client:

Treatment (include testing chakras, aura scan, intention, symbols used, client reactions and so on):

After treatment (include client feedback, advice given, follow-up appointments discussed and so on):

Conclusion:

INDEX